Contenidos

GW01111962

High-frequency words

Common verbs

alcanzar	*to reach*
abrir	*to open*
cerrar	*to close*
comenzar	*to begin*
continuar	*to continue*
corregir	*to correct*
dar	*to give*
dejar de	*to stop (doing something)*
echar	*to throw*
empezar	*to begin*
estar equivocado/a	*to make a mistake / to be wrong*
hacer	*to do / to make*
ir	*to go*
irse	*to go away / to leave*
mentir	*to tell a lie*
necesitar	*to need*
permitir	*to allow*
poner	*to put*
ponerse a	*to start doing something*
prohibir	*to forbid / to ban*
seguir	*to continue / to follow*
tener	*to have / to own*
tener razón	*to be right*

Had a look ☐ **Nearly there** ☐ **Nailed it** ☐

acabar de + infinitive	*to have just (done something)*
deber	*must / to have to*
estar	*to be*
hace(n) falta	*to need / to be necessary*
hacerse	*to become*
hay	*there is / there are*
hay que	*one must / one has to*
ir a + infinitive	*(to be) going to (do something)*
poder	*to be able / can*
ser	*to be*
soler + infinitive	*to regularly do (something)*
tener que + infinitive	*to have to do (something)*
volver a + infinitive	*to do (something) again*
volverse	*to become*

Had a look ☐ **Nearly there** ☐ **Nailed it** ☐

bastar	*to be enough*
durar	*to last*
estar situado/a	*to be situated*
encontrarse	*to be situated*
hace (+ time) …	*it's been …*
medir	*to measure*
mojar(se)	*to get wet*
ocurrir	*to happen*
pasar	*to happen / to go through / to spend (time)*
pesar	*to weigh*
tener (calor / frío)	*to feel (hot / cold)*
tener lugar	*to take place*
tener prisa	*to be in a hurry*
valer la pena	*to be worth the trouble*

Had a look ☐ **Nearly there** ☐ **Nailed it** ☐

adorar	*to adore / to love*
alegrar	*to cheer up*
alegrarse (de)	*to be happy about*
apreciar	*to appreciate*
aprovechar	*to make the most*
aprovecharse (de)	*to take advantage (of)*
desear	*to wish*
disfrutar	*to enjoy*
divertirse	*to have a good time*
encantar	*to delight*
estar a favor de	*to be in favour of*
estar de acuerdo	*to agree*
pasarlo bien / mal	*to have a good / bad time*
querer	*to want / to love*
sentir(se)	*to feel*

Had a look ☐ **Nearly there** ☐ **Nailed it** ☐

creer	*to believe*
darse cuenta (de)	*to realise*
decidir	*to decide*
decir	*to say*
dudar	*to doubt*
esperar	*to hope*
opinar	*to think / to give an opinion*
parecer	*to seem*
pensar	*to think*
ponerse de acuerdo	*to agree*
preferir	*to prefer*
quedar en	*to agree*
querer decir	*to mean*
reconocer	*to recognise*
saber	*to know (a fact / how to do something)*
tener razón	*to be right*

Had a look ☐ **Nearly there** ☐ **Nailed it** ☐

aburrirse	*to get bored*
decepcionar	*to disappoint*
dar igual	*to be all the same / to make no difference*
estar en contra	*to be against*
estar harto/a de	*to be fed up with*
fastidiar	*to annoy / to bother*
odiar	*to hate*

Had a look ☐ **Nearly there** ☐ **Nailed it** ☐

Common adjectives

afortunado/a	*lucky*
agradable	*pleasant*
alucinante	*amazing*
bonito/a	*pretty*
bueno/a	*good*
divertido/a	*amusing / entertaining*
emocionante	*exciting / thrilling / moving*
encantador(a)	*charming*
entretenido/a	*entertaining / amusing*
espléndido/a	*fantastic / great / terrific*
estupendo/a	*fantastic / marvellous*
fenomenal	*great / fantastic*
genial	*brilliant / great*
guay	*cool*
hermoso/a	*beautiful*
maravilloso/a	*marvellous*
impresionante	*impressive / striking*
increíble	*incredible*
precioso/a	*precious / beautiful*

Had a look ☐ **Nearly there** ☐ **Nailed it** ☐

aburrido/a	*boring / bored*
decepcionado/a	*disappointed*
decepcionante	*disappointing*
desagradable	*unpleasant*
fatal	*awful / fatal*
horroroso/a	*horrible*
inseguro	*unsafe / uncertain / insecure*
inútil	*useless*
malo/a	*bad*

Had a look ☐ **Nearly there** ☐ **Nailed it** ☐

abierto/a	*open*
alto/a	*tall / high*
ancho/a	*wide*
antiguo/a	*old*
bajo/a	*low / short*
cerrado/a	*closed*
delgado/a	*slim / thin*
estrecho/a	*narrow*
feo/a	*ugly*
gordo/a	*fat*
grueso/a	*thick*
lleno/a	*full*
nuevo/a	*new*
tonto/a	*silly*
vacío/a	*empty*
viejo/a	*old*

Had a look ☐ **Nearly there** ☐ **Nailed it** ☐

apropiado/a	*correct / appropriate*
barato/a	*cheap*
caro/a	*expensive*
cierto/a	*certain / sure / true*
distinto/a	*different*
duro/a	*hard*
equivocado/a	*wrong*
fácil	*easy*
gratis / gratuito/a	*free (of charge)*
libre	*free / unoccupied*
lento/a	*slow*
mediano/a	*medium*
ocupado/a	*engaged / occupied*
profundo/a	*deep / profound*
raro/a	*strange / rare*
seguro/a	*safe / certain / self-assured*
sencillo/a	*simple / plain / straightforward*
sorprendido/a	*surprised*
tranquilo/a	*peaceful / quiet*
único/a	*unique / only / single*
útil	*useful*

Had a look ☐ **Nearly there** ☐ **Nailed it** ☐

Common adverbs

afortunadamente	*fortunately*
bien	*well*
casi	*almost*
deprisa	*quickly*
desafortunadamente	*unfortunately*
desgraciadamente	*unfortunately*
especialmente	*especially*
inmediatamente	*immediately*
mal	*badly*
más	*more*
no obstante	*nevertheless*
por suerte	*fortunately*
quizás / quizá	*perhaps*
rápidamente	*quickly*
realmente	*really*
recientemente	*recently*
sin embargo	*nevertheless*
sobre todo	*especially*

Had a look ☐ **Nearly there** ☐ **Nailed it** ☐

Prepositions

a	*to / at*
de	*from / of*
en	*in*
hacia	*towards*
hasta	*until*
para	*for*
por	*through / by / in / for / per*
según	*according to*
sin	*without*

Had a look ☐ **Nearly there** ☐ **Nailed it** ☐

Connectives

además	*moreover / besides*
aparte de	*apart from*
claro que	*of course*

dado que	*given that*
es decir	*in other words / that is to say*
por un lado … por otro lado	*on the one hand … on the other hand*
por una parte … por otra parte	*on the one hand … on the other hand*
sin duda	*obviously / certainly / undoubtedly*

Had a look ☐ **Nearly there** ☐ **Nailed it** ☐

Negatives

jamás	*never*
ni … ni	*neither … nor*
nada	*nothing*
nadie	*nobody*
ninguno/a	*none / no one / any / no*
nunca	*never*
sino	*but / except*
tampoco	*neither / not … either …*
ya no	*not any more*

Had a look ☐ **Nearly there** ☐ **Nailed it** ☐

Comparisons / Superlatives

bastante	*sufficient / enough / quite*
demasiado/a	*too / too much*
igual que	*same as*
más (que)	*more (than)*
mayor	*main / major / larger / bigger / greater*
la mayoría	*most / majority*
mejor	*better / best*
menor	*smaller / less / least*
menos (que)	*less (than)*
mismo/a	*same*
muy	*very*
parecido/a a	*like / similar to*
peor	*worse / worst*
poco (ruidoso)	*not very (noisy)*
tan … como	*as … as*
tanto/a … como	*as much … as*

Had a look ☐ **Nearly there** ☐ **Nailed it** ☐

Conjunctions

a pesar de	*in spite of / despite*
así que	*so / therefore*
aun (cuando)	*even (if)*
aunque	*although / (even) though*
como	*as / since*
cuando	*when*
incluso	*even*
mientras (que)	*while / meanwhile*
o/u	*or*
pero	*but*
por eso	*for that reason / therefore*
por lo tanto	*therefore*
porque	*because*
pues	*then / since*
si	*if*
sin embargo	*however*
tal vez	*maybe / perhaps*
también	*also*
ya que	*as / since*

Had a look ☐ **Nearly there** ☐ **Nailed it** ☐

Question words

¿(a)dónde?	*where?*
¿cómo?	*how?*
¿cuál(es)?	*which?*
¿cuándo?	*when?*
¿cuánto/a?	*how much?*
¿cuántos/as …?	*how many?*
¿de dónde?	*where from?*
¿de quién?	*whose?*
¿por dónde?	*through where?*
¿por qué?	*why?*
¿qué?	*what?*
¿quién?	*who?*

Had a look ☐ **Nearly there** ☐ **Nailed it** ☐

¿a qué hora?	*at what time?*
¿cuánto cuesta(n)?	*how much does it / do they cost?*
¿cuánto es?	*how much is it?*
¿cuánto vale(n)?	*how much does it / do they cost?*
¿cuántos años tiene(s)?	*how old are you?*
¿de qué color?	*what colour?*
¿para / por cuánto tiempo?	*for how long?*
¿qué día?	*what day?*
¿qué fecha?	*what date?*
¿qué hora es?	*what time is it?*

Had a look ☐ **Nearly there** ☐ **Nailed it** ☐

Time expressions

a la una	*at one o'clock*
a las dos, etc.	*at two o'clock, etc.*
y cinco, etc.	*five past, etc.*
y cuarto	*quarter past*
y media	*half past*
menos cuarto	*quarter to*
menos diez, etc.	*ten to, etc.*
de la mañana	*in the morning*
de la tarde	*in the afternoon / in the evening*
es la una	*it's one o'clock*
son las dos, etc.	*it's two o'clock, etc.*
la hora	*hour*
el minuto	*minute*
la medianoche	*midnight*
el mediodía	*noon*

Had a look ☐ **Nearly there** ☐ **Nailed it** ☐

el año	*year*
anoche	*last night*
ayer	*yesterday*
el día	*day*
el fin de semana	*weekend*
el mes	*month*
la estación	*season*
esta noche	*tonight*
hoy	*today*
la fecha	*date*
la mañana	*morning*
la noche	*night*
la semana	*week*
la tarde	*afternoon / evening*
mañana	*tomorrow*
pasado mañana	*day after tomorrow*
quince días	*fortnight*
el rato	*while / short time*
el pasado	*past*
el porvenir	*future*

Had a look ☐ **Nearly there** ☐ **Nailed it** ☐

Days, months and seasons of the year

lunes	*Monday*
martes	*Tuesday*
miércoles	*Wednesday*
jueves	*Thursday*
viernes	*Friday*
sábado	*Saturday*
domingo	*Sunday*
(el) lunes	*(on) Monday*
(el) lunes por la mañana	*(on) Monday morning*
(el) lunes por la tarde	*(on) Monday evening*
los lunes	*on Mondays*
cada lunes	*every Monday*

Had a look ☐ **Nearly there** ☐ **Nailed it** ☐

enero	*January*
febrero	*February*
marzo	*March*
abril	*April*
mayo	*May*
junio	*June*
julio	*July*
agosto	*August*
septiembre	*September*
octubre	*October*
noviembre	*November*
diciembre	*December*

Had a look ☐ **Nearly there** ☐ **Nailed it** ☐

la primavera	*spring*
el verano	*summer*
el otoño	*autumn*
el invierno	*winter*

Had a look ☐ **Nearly there** ☐ **Nailed it** ☐

Frequency expressions

a diario	*daily / everyday*
a eso de …	*at about …*
a mediados de …	*around the middle of …*
a menudo	*often*
a partir de	*from*
a veces	*sometimes*
ahora	*now / nowadays*
al mismo tiempo	*at the same time*
algunas veces	*sometimes*
antes (de)	*before*
cada (…) días / horas	*every (…) days / hours*
de vez en cuando	*now and then / from time to time*
dentro de (…) días / horas	*within (…) days / hours*
desde / desde hace	*since*
después (de)	*after / afterwards*
durante	*during*
en seguida / enseguida	*straightaway*
entonces	*then*
luego	*then / afterwards*
mientras tanto	*meanwhile*

Had a look ☐ **Nearly there** ☐ **Nailed it** ☐

de momento	*at the moment / right now*
de nuevo	*again*
otra vez	*again*
de repente	*suddenly*
(por) mucho tiempo	*(for) a long time*
pocas veces	*seldom / a few times*
por fin	*at last*
al principio	*at the beginning*
pronto	*soon*
próximo/a	*next*
que viene (el mes, etc.)	*next (month, etc.)*
siempre	*always*
siguiente	*next / following*
sobre	*on / around*
tarde	*late*
temprano	*early*
todos/as (las semanas / los días / meses)	*every (week / day / month)*
todavía	*still / yet*
último/a	*last*
una vez (dos / tres veces, etc.)	*once (twice / three times, etc.)*
ya	*already*

Had a look ☐ **Nearly there** ☐ **Nailed it** ☐

Location and distance

abajo (de)	*under / below*
afuera (de)	*outside*
ahí	*there*
allá	*over there*
allí	*over there*

atrás	*behind*
delante (de)	*in front of*
detrás (de)	*behind*
cerca (de)	*near*
enfrente (de)	*opposite*
entre	*between*
a la derecha / izquierda	*on the / to the right / left*
a mano derecha / izquierda	*on the right / left*
a un paso (de)	*a few steps away*
al final (de)	*at the end of*
al lado (de)	*next to*
en la esquina	*on the corner*
todo recto	*straight on / ahead*

Had a look ☐ **Nearly there** ☐ **Nailed it** ☐

alrededor (de)	*around*
aquí	*here*
arriba (de)	*above / on top (of)*
cercano/a	*nearby*
contra	*against*
debajo (de)	*under*
dentro (de)	*inside*
en el medio (de)	*in the middle of*
en / por todas partes	*everywhere*
en las afueras	*in the outskirts*
encima (de)	*above / on top / overhead*
el este	*east*
en el / al fondo	*at the back / at the bottom*
fuera (de)	*outside*
lejos (de)	*far (from)*
el lugar	*place*
el norte	*north*
el oeste	*west*
el sitio	*place*
el sur	*south*

Had a look ☐ **Nearly there** ☐ **Nailed it** ☐

Numbers

uno	*1*
dos	*2*
tres	*3*
cuatro	*4*
cinco	*5*
seis	*6*
siete	*7*
ocho	*8*
nueve	*9*
diez	*10*
once	*11*
doce	*12*
trece	*13*
catorce	*14*
quince	*15*
dieciséis	*16*
diecisiete	*17*
dieciocho	*18*
diecinueve	*19*
veinte	*20*

Had a look ☐ **Nearly there** ☐ **Nailed it** ☐

veintiuno	*21*
veintidós	*22*
veintitrés	*23*
veinticuatro	*24*
veinticinco	*25*
veintiséis	*26*
veintisiete	*27*
veintiocho	*28*
veintinueve	*29*
treinta	*30*

Had a look ☐ **Nearly there** ☐ **Nailed it** ☐

cuarenta	*40*
cincuenta	*50*
sesenta	*60*
setenta	*70*
ochenta	*80*
noventa	*90*
cien(to)	*100*
ciento uno/a	*101*
doscientos/as	*200*
mil	*1,000*
mil cien(to)	*1,100*
dos mil	*2,000*
(un) millón (de)	*1,000,000*

Had a look ☐ **Nearly there** ☐ **Nailed it** ☐

primer / primero/a	*first*
segundo/a	*second*
tercer / tercero/a	*third*
cuarto/a	*fourth*
quinto/a	*fifth*
sexto/a	*sixth*
séptimo/a	*seventh*
octavo/a	*eighth*
noveno/a	*ninth*
décimo/a	*tenth*

Had a look ☐ **Nearly there** ☐ **Nailed it** ☐

mil novecientos noventa y cinco	*1995*
dos mil diecisiete	*2017*
(una) docena	*dozen*
el número	*number*
un par	*pair / couple*
unos/as (diez)	*about (10)*

Had a look ☐ **Nearly there** ☐ **Nailed it** ☐

Colours

amarillo/a	*yellow*
azul	*blue*
blanco/a	*white*
castaño/a	*chestnut brown*
claro/a	*light*
el color	*colour*
gris	*grey*
marrón	*brown*
morado/a / violeta	*purple / violet*
moreno/a	*dark (hair / skin)*
naranja	*orange*
negro	*black*
oscuro/a	*dark*
pálido/a	*pale*
rojo/a	*red*
rosa / rosado/a	*pink*
rubio/a	*fair (hair / skin)*
verde	*green*
vivo/a	*vivid / bright*

Had a look ☐ **Nearly there** ☐ **Nailed it** ☐

Weather

el cielo	*sky*
el clima	*climate*
el chubasco	*shower*
la lluvia	*rain*
la niebla	*fog*
la nieve	*snow*
la nube	*cloud*
el pronóstico	*forecast*
el relámpago	*lightning*
el grado	*degree*
el hielo	*ice*
el tiempo	*weather*
la tormenta	*storm*
el trueno	*thunder*
el viento	*wind*

Had a look ☐ **Nearly there** ☐ **Nailed it** ☐

caliente	*hot*
caluroso	*hot / warm*
despejado	*clear (skies)*
estable	*stable / steady / unchanged*
fresco	*fresh*
húmedo	*humid*
nublado / nuboso	*cloudy*
seco	*dry*
la sombra	*shade / shadow*
templado	*mild / temperate*
tormentoso	*stormy*
buen / mal tiempo	*good / bad weather*
hacer (frío / calor / etc.)	*to be (cold / hot / etc.)*
helar	*to freeze*
llover	*to rain*
mojar(se)	*to get wet*
nevar	*to snow*
tener (calor / frío)	*to feel (hot / cold)*

Had a look ☐ **Nearly there** ☐ **Nailed it** ☐

Weights, measures and containers

la altura	*height*
el ancho / la anchura	*width*
la bolsa	*bag*
el bote	*jar*
la caja	*box*
la cantidad	*quantity*
el cartón	*carton*
un cuarto	*quarter*
la lata	*tin*
la medida	*measure*
medio	*half*
la mitad	*half*
el pedazo	*piece*
el peso	*weight*
un poco	*little*
la ración	*portion*
la talla	*size (clothes)*
el tamaño	*size*
el trozo	*piece*

Had a look ☐ **Nearly there** ☐ **Nailed it** ☐

Countries and continents

Alemania	*Germany*
Austria	*Austria*
Bélgica	*Belgium*
Dinamarca	*Denmark*
Escocia	*Scotland*
España	*Spain*
Francia	*France*
Gran Bretaña	*Great Britain*
Grecia	*Greece*
Holanda	*Holland*
Inglaterra	*England*
Irlanda	*Ireland*
Italia	*Italy*
(País de) Gales	*Wales*
Países Bajos	*Netherlands*
Reino Unido	*United Kingdom*
Suecia	*Sweden*
Suiza	*Switzerland*
Turquía	*Turkey*

Had a look ☐ **Nearly there** ☐ **Nailed it** ☐

Argentina	*Argentina*
Brasil	*Brazil*
Estados Unidos	*United States*
India	*India*
México	*Mexico*
Pakistán	*Pakistan*

Perú	*Peru*
Rusia	*Russia*

Had a look ☐ **Nearly there** ☐ **Nailed it** ☐

África	*Africa*
América del Norte / Norteamérica	*North America*
América del Sur / Sudamérica	*South America*
América Latina / Latinoamérica	*Latin America*
Asia	*Asia*
Australia	*Australia*
Europa	*Europe*

Had a look ☐ **Nearly there** ☐ **Nailed it** ☐

Nationalities

alemán/alemana	*German*
austriaco/a	*Austrian*
belga	*Belgian*
británico/a	*British*
danés/danesa	*Danish*
escocés/escocesa	*Scottish*
español/a	*Spanish*
europeo/a	*European*
francés/francesa	*French*
galés/galesa	*Welsh*
griego/a	*Greek*
holandés/holandesa	*Dutch*
inglés/inglesa	*English*
irlandés/irlandesa	*Irish*
italiano/a	*Italian*
sueco/a	*Swedish*
suizo/a	*Swiss*
turco/a	*Turkish*

Had a look ☐ **Nearly there** ☐ **Nailed it** ☐

americano/a	*American*
argentino/a	*Argentinian*
boliviano/a	*Bolivian*
brasileño/a	*Brazilian*
chileno/a	*Chilean*
chino/a	*Chinese*
colombiano/a	*Colombian*
ecuatoriano/a	*Ecuadorean*
indio/a	*Indian*
italiano/a	*Italian*
japonés/japonesa	*Japanese*
mexicano/a	*Mexican*
pakistaní	*Pakistani*
peruano/a	*Peruvian*
ruso/a	*Russian*
venezolano/a	*Venezuelan*

Had a look ☐ **Nearly there** ☐ **Nailed it** ☐

Areas, mountains and seas

Andalucía	*Andalusia*
Aragón	*Aragon*
el canal de la Mancha	*the English Channel*
Castilla	*Castile*
Cataluña	*Catalonia*
comunidades autónomas	*autonomous communities*
Galicia	*Galicia*
el mar Cantábrico	*Cantabrian Sea*
el mar Mediterráneo	*Mediterranean Sea*
el océano Atlántico	*Atlantic Ocean*
(el) País Vasco	*(the) Basque Country*
los Pirineos	*the Pyrenees*
La Rioja	*Rioja*

Had a look ☐ **Nearly there** ☐ **Nailed it** ☐

Materials

el algodón	*cotton*
la cerámica	*pottery*
el cristal	*glass / crystal*
el cuero	*leather*
la lana	*wool*
la madera	*wood*
el oro	*gold*
el papel	*paper*
la piel	*leather / skin*
la plata	*silver*
la seda	*silk*
la tela	*fabric / material*
el vidrio	*glass*

Had a look ☐ **Nearly there** ☐ **Nailed it** ☐

Greetings and exclamations

¿Cómo está(s)?	*How are you?*
¿De veras?	*Really?*
con permiso	*excuse me*
de nada	*you're welcome / don't mention it*
encantado/a	*pleased to meet you*
hasta el (lunes)	*till / see you (Monday)*
hasta luego	*see you later*
hasta mañana	*see you tomorrow*
hasta pronto	*see you soon*
lo siento	*I'm sorry*
mucho gusto	*pleased to meet you*
perdón	*sorry*
perdone	*sorry*
por favor	*please*
¡Que lo pase(s) bien!	*Have a good time!*
¿Qué hay?	*What's happening? / What's the matter?*
¿Qué pasa?	*What's happening? / What's the matter?*
¿Qué tal?	*How are you? / How's …?*
saludar	*to greet / to say hello*

saludos	*regards / greetings*
vale	*OK*

Had a look ☐ **Nearly there** ☐ **Nailed it** ☐

¡Basta ya!	*That's enough!*
¡Bienvenido/a!	*Welcome!*
¡Buen viaje!	*Have a good trip!*
¡Buena suerte!	*Good luck!*
¡Claro!	*Of course!*
¡Cuidado!	*Careful! / Watch out!*
¡Enhorabuena!	*Congratulations!*
¡Felices vacaciones!	*Have a good holiday!*
¡Felicidades!	*Best wishes! / Congratulations!*
¡Felicitaciones!	*Congratulations!*
¡Ojo!	*Watch out! / Careful!*
¡Qué (+ adjective)!	*How …!*
¡Qué (+ noun)!	*What a …!*
¡Que suerte!	*What luck!*
¡Qué va!	*Come on! / Rubbish! / Nonsense!*
¡Socorro!	*Help!*

Had a look ☐ **Nearly there** ☐ **Nailed it** ☐

Language used in dialogues and messages

a la atención de	*for the attention of*
el auricular	*receiver (telephone)*
con relación a	*further to / following*
de momento	*at the moment*
en contacto con	*in communication with*
enviado/a por	*sent by*
escucho / dígame	*I'm listening*
espere	*wait*
hablando / al aparato / en la línea	*on the line / speaking*
le paso	*I will put you through*
llámame (informal) / llámeme (formal)	*call me (informal / formal)*
marcar el número	*dial the number*
el mensaje (de texto)	*text message*
el mensaje en el contestador	*voice mail*
no cuelgue	*stay on the line*
el número equivocado	*wrong number*
el prefijo	*area code*
el teléfono	*telephone*
el texto	*text*
el timbre / el tono	*tone*
vuelvo enseguida	*I'll be right back*

Had a look ☐ **Nearly there** ☐ **Nailed it** ☐

Other useful expressions

aquí lo tiene(s)	*here you are*
buena suerte	*good luck*
¿Cómo se escribe?	*How do you spell that?*
con (mucho) gusto / placer	*with pleasure*
de acuerdo	*OK (I agree)*
depende	*it depends*
en mi opinión	*in my opinion*
estoy bien	*I'm fine*
gracias	*thank you*
he tenido bastante	*I've had enough*
me da igual	*I don't mind*
menos mal	*just as well*
mío/a	*mine*
no importa	*it doesn't matter*
otra vez	*once again*
por supuesto	*of course*
por si acaso	*just in case*
qué lástima / qué pena	*what a shame*
ten (informal) / tenga (formal)	*there you are (informal / formal)*

Had a look ☐ **Nearly there** ☐ **Nailed it** ☐

Other useful words

algo	*something*
alguien	*someone*
la cifra	*figure*
como	*as / like*
la cosa	*thing*
la desventaja	*disadvantage*
todo el mundo	*everybody*
todos	*everybody*
eso/a/os/as	*that / those*
esto/a/os/as	*this / these*

Had a look ☐ **Nearly there** ☐ **Nailed it** ☐

la falta	*error*
la forma	*shape*
la forma	*way*
la manera	*way*
el género	*type / kind / sort*
el tipo	*type / kind / sort*
el medio	*middle*
la mitad	*half*
no	*no*
el número	*number*
por ejemplo	*for example*
la razón	*reason*
señor	*Mr*
señora	*Mrs*
señorita	*Miss*
si	*if*
sí	*yes*
la ventaja	*advantage*
la verdad	*truth*

Had a look ☐ **Nearly there** ☐ **Nailed it** ☐

Words I should know for speaking and writing activities

¿Dónde vives?	***Where do you live?***
Vivo en el …	*I live in the …*
norte / noreste / noroeste …	*north / northeast / northwest …*
sur / sureste / suroeste …	*south / southeast / southwest …*
este / oeste / centro …	*east / west / centre …*
de Inglaterra / Escocia	*of England / Scotland*
de Gales / Irlanda (del Norte)	*of Wales / (Northern) Ireland*

Had a look ☐ **Nearly there** ☐ **Nailed it** ☐

¿Qué haces en verano?	***What do you do in summer?***
En verano / invierno …	*In summer / winter …*
chateo en la red	*I chat online*
cocino para mi familia	*I cook for my family*
descargo canciones	*I download songs*
escribo correos	*I write emails*
hago natación / esquí / windsurf	*I go swimming / skiing / windsurfing*
hago una barbacoa	*I have a barbecue*
juego al baloncesto / fútbol	*I play basketball / football*
monto a caballo / en bici	*I go horseriding / cycling*
nado en el mar	*I swim in the sea*
salgo con mis amigos/as	*I go out with my friends*
toco la guitarra	*I play the guitar*
trabajo como voluntario/a	*I work as a volunteer*
veo la tele	*I watch TV*
voy al polideportivo / al parque / a un centro comercial	*I go to the sports centre / to the park / to a shopping centre*
voy de paseo	*I go for a walk*

Had a look ☐ **Nearly there** ☐ **Nailed it** ☐

¿Con qué frecuencia?	***How often?***
siempre	*always*
a menudo	*often*
todos los días	*every day*
a veces	*sometimes*
de vez en cuando	*from time to time*
una vez a la semana	*once a week*
dos o tres veces al año	*two or three times a year*
(casi) nunca	*(almost) never*

Had a look ☐ **Nearly there** ☐ **Nailed it** ☐

¿Qué tiempo hace?	***What's the weather like?***
Hace buen / mal tiempo.	*It's good / bad weather.*
Hace calor / frío / sol / viento.	*It's hot / cold / sunny / windy.*
Llueve / Nieva.	*It's raining / snowing.*
El tiempo es variable.	*The weather is changeable.*
El clima es caluroso / soleado.	*The climate is hot / sunny.*
Hay niebla / tormenta.	*It's foggy / stormy.*
Hay chubascos.	*There are showers.*
Está nublado.	*It's cloudy.*

Had a look ☐ **Nearly there** ☐ **Nailed it** ☐

¿Qué te gusta hacer?	***What do you like doing?***
Soy adicto/a a …	*I'm addicted to …*
Soy un(a) fanático/a de … ya que / dado que / puesto que …	*I'm a … fan / fanatic … given that / since …*
Prefiero …	*I prefer …*
Me gusta …	*I like …*
Me encanta / Me mola / Me chifla / Me flipa / Me apasiona …	*I love …*

Had a look ☐ **Nearly there** ☐ **Nailed it** ☐

No me gusta (nada) …	*I don't like … (at all)*
Odio …	*I hate …*
A (mi padre) le gusta …	*(My dad) likes …*
Nos encanta …	*We love …*
bucear	*diving*
estar al aire libre	*being outdoors*
estar en contacto con los amigos	*being in touch with friends*
hacer artes marciales	*doing martial arts*
hacer deportes acuáticos	*doing water sports*
ir al cine / a la pista de hielo	*going to the cinema / ice rink*
ir de compras	*going shopping*
leer (un montón de revistas)	*reading (loads of magazines)*
usar el ordenador	*using the computer*
ver películas	*watching films*
Prefiero veranear …	*I prefer to spend the summer …*
en el extranjero / en España	*abroad / in Spain*
en la costa / en el campo	*on the coast / in the country*
en la montaña / en la ciudad	*in the mountains / in the city*

Had a look ☐ **Nearly there** ☐ **Nailed it** ☐

¿Adónde fuiste de vacaciones?	***Where did you go on holiday?***
hace una semana / un mes / un año	*a week / month / year ago*
hace dos semanas / meses / años	*two weeks / months / years ago*
fui de vacaciones a …	*I went on holiday to …*
Francia / Italia / Turquía	*France / Italy / Turkey*
¿Con quién fuiste?	*Who did you go with?*
Fui …	*I went …*
con mi familia / insti	*with my family / school*
con mi mejor amigo/a	*with my best friend*

solo/a	*alone*
¿Cómo viajaste?	*How did you travel?*
Viajé …	*I travelled …*
en autocar / avión	*by coach / plane*
en barco / coche / tren	*by boat / car / train*

Had a look ☐ **Nearly there** ☐ **Nailed it** ☐

¿Qué hiciste?	***What did you do?***
primero	*first*
luego	*then*
más tarde	*later*
después	*after*
finalmente	*finally*
Lo mejor fue cuando …	*The best thing was when …*
Lo peor fue cuando …	*The worst thing was when …*

Had a look ☐ **Nearly there** ☐ **Nailed it** ☐

aprendí a hacer vela	*I learned to sail*
comí muchos helados	*I ate lots of ice creams*
compré recuerdos	*I bought souvenirs*
descansé	*I rested*
fui al acuario	*I went to the aquarium*
hice turismo	*I went sightseeing*
llegué tarde al aeropuerto	*I arrived at the airport late*
perdí mi móvil	*I lost my mobile*
saqué fotos	*I took photos*
tomé el sol	*I sunbathed*
tuve un accidente en la playa	*I had an accident on the beach*
vi un partido	*I saw / watched a match*
visité el Park Güell	*I visited Park Güell*
vomité en una montaña rusa	*I was sick on a roller coaster*
Puedes …	*You can …*
descubrir el Museo Picasso	*discover the Picasso Museum*
disfrutar del Barrio Gótico	*enjoy the Gothic quarter*
pasear por las Ramblas	*walk along Las Ramblas*
subir al Monumento a Colón	*go up the Columbus Monument*
ver los barcos en el puerto	*see the boats in the port*

Had a look ☐ **Nearly there** ☐ **Nailed it** ☐

¿Qué tal lo pasaste?	***How was it?***
Me gustó / Me encantó.	*I liked it / I loved it.*
Lo pasé bomba / fenomenal.	*I had a great time.*
Lo pasé bien / mal / fatal.	*I had a good / bad / awful time.*
Fue …	*It was …*
inolvidable / increíble	*unforgettable / incredible*
impresionante / flipante	*impressive / awesome*
horroroso	*awful*
un desastre	*a disaster*
¿Qué tiempo hizo?	*What was the weather like?*
Hizo buen / mal tiempo.	*It was good / bad weather.*
Hizo calor / frío / sol / viento.	*It was hot / cold / sunny / windy.*
Hubo niebla / tormenta.	*It was foggy / stormy.*
Llovió / Nevó.	*It rained / snowed.*

Had a look ☐ **Nearly there** ☐ **Nailed it** ☐

¿Cómo era el hotel?	***What was the hotel like?***
Me alojé / Me quedé …	*I stayed …*
Nos alojamos / Nos quedamos …	*We stayed …*
en un albergue juvenil	*in a youth hostel*
en un apartamento	*in an apartment*
en un camping	*on a campsite*
en un hotel de cinco estrellas	*in a five-star hotel*
en un parador	*in a state-run luxury hotel*
en una casa rural	*in a house in the country*
en una pensión	*in a guest house*
Fui de crucero.	*I went on a cruise.*
Estaba …	*It was …*
cerca de la playa	*near the beach*
en el centro de la ciudad	*in the city centre*
en las afueras	*on the outskirts*

Had a look ☐ **Nearly there** ☐ **Nailed it** ☐

Era …	*It was …*
acogedor(a)	*welcoming*
antiguo/a	*old*
barato/a	*cheap*
caro/a	*expensive*
grande	*big*
lujoso/a	*luxurious*
moderno/a	*modern*
pequeño/a	*small*
ruidoso/a	*noisy*
tranquilo/a	*quiet*
Tenía / Había …	*It had / There was / were …*
No tenía ni … ni …	*It had neither … nor …*
No había ni … ni …	*There was no … nor …*
Tampoco tenía …	*Nor did it have …*
(un) aparcamiento	*a car park*
(un) bar	*a bar*
(un) gimnasio	*a gym*
(un) restaurante	*a restaurant*
(una) cafetería	*a café*
(una) lavandería	*a launderette*
(una) piscina cubierta	*an indoor pool*
mucho espacio para mi tienda	*lots of space for my tent*

Had a look ☐ **Nearly there** ☐ **Nailed it** ☐

M 1

¿Cómo era el pueblo?	*What was the town / village like?*
Lo bueno / Lo malo …	*The good thing / The bad thing …*
del pueblo …	*about the town / village …*
de la ciudad …	*about the city …*
era que era …	*was that it was …*
demasiado / muy / bastante …	*too / very / quite …*
animado/a	*lively*
bonito/a	*pretty*
histórico/a	*historic*
pintoresco/a	*picturesque*
turístico/a	*touristic*
Tenía …	*It had …*
mucho ambiente / tráfico	*lots of atmosphere / traffic*
mucho que hacer	*lots to do*
mucha contaminación / gente	*lots of pollution / people*
muchos espacios verdes	*lots of green spaces*
muchos lugares de interés	*lots of places of interest*
muchas discotecas	*lots of discos*

Had a look ☐ **Nearly there** ☐ **Nailed it** ☐

Quisiera reservar …	*I would like to book …*
¿Hay …	*Is / Are there …*
wifi gratis …	*free wifi …*
aire acondicionado …	*air conditioning …*
en el hotel / las habitaciones?	*in the hotel / the rooms?*
¿Cuánto cuesta una habitación …?	*How much does a … room cost?*
¿A qué hora se sirve el desayuno?	*What time is breakfast served?*
¿Cuándo está abierto/a el/la …?	*When is the … open?*
¿Cuánto es el suplemento por …?	*How much is the supplement for …?*
¿Se admiten perros?	*Are dogs allowed?*
Quisiera reservar …	*I would like to book …*
una habitación individual / doble	*a single / double room*
con / sin balcón	*with / without a balcony*
con bañera / ducha	*with a bath / shower*
con cama de matrimonio	*with a double bed*
con desayuno incluido	*with breakfast included*
con media pensión	*with half board*
con pensión completa	*with full board*
con vistas al mar	*with a sea view*
¿Para cuántas noches?	*For how many nights?*
Para … noches	*For … nights*
del … al … de …	*from the … to the … of …*
¿Puede repetir, por favor?	*Can you repeat, please?*
¿Puede hablar más despacio?	*Can you speak more slowly?*

Had a look ☐ **Nearly there** ☐ **Nailed it** ☐

Quiero quejarme	*I want to complain*
Quiero hablar con el director.	*I want to speak to the manager.*
Quiero cambiar de habitación.	*I want to change rooms.*
La ducha / La habitación …	*The shower / The room …*
está sucio/a	*is dirty*
El ascensor / La luz / El aire acondicionado …	*The lift / The light / The air conditioning …*
no funciona	*doesn't work*
Hay ratas en la cama.	*There are rats in the bed.*
No hay …	*There is no …*
Necesito …	*I need …*
papel higiénico	*toilet paper*
jabón / champú	*soap / shampoo*
toallas / (un) secador	*towels / a hairdryer*
¡Socorro!	*Help!*
Es inaceptable.	*It's unacceptable.*
Lo siento / Perdone.	*I'm sorry.*
El hotel está completo.	*The hotel is full.*

Had a look ☐ **Nearly there** ☐ **Nailed it** ☐

Mis vacaciones desastrosas	*My disastrous holiday*
Por desgracia	*Unfortunately*
Por un lado … por otro lado …	*On one hand … on the other hand …*
El primer / último día	*(On) the first / last day*
Al día siguiente	*On the following day*
Tuve / Tuvimos …	*I had / We had …*
un accidente / un pinchazo	*an accident / a puncture*
un retraso / una avería	*a delay / a breakdown*
Tuve / Tuvimos que …	*I had to / We had to …*
esperar mucho tiempo	*wait a long time*
ir al hospital / a la comisaría	*go to the hospital / to the police station*
llamar a un mecánico	*call a mechanic*
Perdí / Perdimos …	*I lost / We lost …*
el equipaje / la cartera	*the luggage / the wallet*
la maleta / las llaves	*the suitcase / the keys*

Had a look ☐ **Nearly there** ☐ **Nailed it** ☐

Cuando llegamos …	*When we arrived …*
era muy tarde	*it was very late*
estaba cansado/a	*I was tired*
la recepción ya estaba cerrada	*the reception was already closed*
acampar	*to camp*
decidir	*to decide (to)*
alquilar bicicletas	*to hire bicycles*
coger el teleférico	*to catch / take the cable car*
chocar con	*to crash into*
hacer alpinismo	*to go mountain climbing*
volver	*to return*
el paisaje	*the landscape*
la autopista	*the motorway*
precioso/a	*beautiful*

Had a look ☐ **Nearly there** ☐ **Nailed it** ☐

Extra words I should know for reading and listening activities

¿Qué haces en tu tiempo libre?	***What do you do in your free time?***
la canoa	*canoe*
el centro comercial	*shopping centre*
chatear en la red	*to communicate on the internet*
descansar	*to relax*
echar relajo	*to go wild (Mexican slang)*
escalada	*climbing*
hacer alpinismo	*to go mountain climbing*
hacer deportes acuáticos	*to do water sports*
hacer / practicar deporte	*to do sport*
ir de compras	*to go shopping*
ir de paseo	*to go for a walk*
el montón de revistas	*pile of magazines*
la pista comando	*assault course*
la pista de hielo	*ice rink*
el refugio de animales	*animal sanctuary*
ser un/a líder	*to be a leader*
el taller creativo / de cocina / teatro / etc.	*creative / cookery / theatre etc. workshop*
el tiro con arco	*archery*
trabajar en equipo	*to work in a team*
usar el ordenador	*to go on the computer*

Had a look ☐ **Nearly there** ☐ **Nailed it** ☐

¿Qué haces cuando vas de vacaciones?	***What you do when you go on holiday?***
¿Adónde fuiste de vacaciones el año pasado?	*Where did you go on holiday last year?*
¿Dónde pasaste tus últimas vacaciones?	*Where did you go on your last holiday?*
broncearse	*to get a tan*
bucear	*to swim underwater / to scuba dive*
estar al aire libre	*to be outside*
hacer manualidades	*to do handicrafts*
hacer turismo	*to do tourism*
el helado	*ice cream*
inscribirse	*to enroll*
la insolación	*sunstroke*
nadar	*to swim*
el paisaje	*landscape / scenery*
el paraguas*	*umbrella*
pegar (el sol)	*the beat down (of the sun)*
el recorrido	*tour*
el recuerdo	*souvenir*
sacar fotos**	*to take photos*
la sombrilla	*sunshade / parasol*
tomar el sol	*to sunbathe*

Had a look ☐ **Nearly there** ☐ **Nailed it** ☐

¿Cómo viajas y dónde te alojas?	***How do you travel and where do you stay?***
acampar	*to camp*
acogedor(a)	*friendly / welcoming / cosy*
el albergue juvenil	*youth hostel*
alejado de la civilización	*far from civilisation*
alojarse / quedarse	*to stay*
alquilar un apartamento / una casa	*to rent an apartment / a house*
el campamento de verano	*summer camp*
ir al extranjero	*to go abroad*
ir de crucero	*to go on a cruise*
llegar pronto / tarde	*to arrive early / late*
el parador	*state-run luxury hotel*
Quisiera reservar una habitación.	*I would like to reserve a room.*
recorrer a pie	*to explore on foot*
el retraso	*delay*
tener un accidente / un pinchazo	*to have an accident / a puncture*
tener una avería	*to break down*
el trayecto	*journey*
viajar en coche / avión / barco / tren / autocar	*to travel by car / plane / boat / train / coach*

Had a look ☐ **Nearly there** ☐ **Nailed it** ☐

***Work out the meaning of unfamiliar words**

When trying to work out the meaning of a word look for clues. *El paraguas* combines the words *para* and *agua*, which would literally translate 'for water'. Note too that although *paraguas* ends with 's' it is a singular noun so you would say, for example, *¿Dónde está mi paraguas?*

****Pick the right verb**

Don't fall into the trap of using *tomar* when you want to say 'to take a photo'. The correct verbs to use in Spanish are *sacar* or *hacer*. Example: *Siempre saco / hago muchas fotos cuando voy de vacaciones.*

M 2

Words I should know for speaking and writing activities

¿Te interesa(n) ...?	***Are you interested in ...?***
el arte dramático	*drama*
el dibujo	*art / drawing*
el español	*Spanish*
el inglés	*English*
la biología	*biology*
la educación física	*PE*
la física	*physics*
la geografía	*geography*
la historia	*history*
la informática	*ICT*
la lengua	*language*
la química	*chemistry*
la religión	*RE*
la tecnología	*technology*
los idiomas	*languages*
las empresariales	*business studies*
las matemáticas	*maths*
las ciencias	*science*
la materia / la asignatura	*subject*

Had a look ☐ **Nearly there** ☐ **Nailed it** ☐

me encanta(n) / me chifla(n)	*I love*
me interesa(n) / me fascina(n)	*I'm interested in / fascinated by*
me gusta(n) / no me gusta(n)	*I like / I don't like*
odio	*I hate*
prefiero	*I prefer*
porque es / son	*because it is / they are*
Mi día preferido es (el viernes).	*My favourite day is (Friday).*
mi horario	*my timetable*
¿Qué día tienes ...?	*What day do you have ...?*
Tengo inglés los martes.	*I have English on Tuesdays.*
¿A qué hora tienes ...?	*What time do you have ...?*
a la una / a las dos	*at one o'clock / at two o'clock*
y / menos cuarto	*quarter past / to*
y / menos cinco	*five past / to*
y media	*half past*
la educación infantil / primaria	*pre-school / primary education*
la educación secundaria	*secondary education*
el bachillerato	*A levels*
la formación profesional	*vocational training*
el instituto	*secondary school*

Had a look ☐ **Nearly there** ☐ **Nailed it** ☐

¿Qué tal los estudios?	***How are your studies?***
La física es más / menos ... que ...	*Physics is more / less ... than ...*
Es mejor / peor que ...	*It's better / worse than ...*
tan ... como	*as ... as*
fácil / difícil	*easy / difficult*
divertido/a / aburrido/a	*fun / boring*
útil / relevante / práctico/a	*useful / relevant / practical*
creativo/a / relajante	*creative / relaxing*
exacto/a / lógico/a	*precise / logical*
exigente	*demanding*
Mi profesor(a) (de ciencias) es ...	*My (science) teacher is ...*
paciente / impaciente	*patient / impatient*
tolerante / severo/a	*tolerant / harsh*
listo/a / tonto/a	*clever / stupid*
trabajador(a)	*hard-working*
perezoso/a	*lazy*
simpático/a / estricto/a	*nice / strict*

Had a look ☐ **Nearly there** ☐ **Nailed it** ☐

Mi profe ...	*My teacher ...*
enseña / explica bien	*teaches / explains well*
tiene buen sentido de humor	*has a good sense of humour*
tiene expectativas altas	*has high expectations*
crea un buen ambiente de trabajo	*creates a good working atmosphere*
nunca se enfada	*never gets angry*
me hace pensar	*makes me think*
nos da consejos / estrategias	*gives us advice / strategies*
nos pone muchos deberes	*gives us lots of homework*
el curso académico	*academic year*
las pruebas / las evaluaciones	*tests / assessments*
suspender / aprobar	*to fail / to pass*

Had a look ☐ **Nearly there** ☐ **Nailed it** ☐

¿Cómo es tu insti?	***What is your school like?***
En mi instituto hay ...	*In my school there is ...*
Mi instituto tiene ...	*My school has ...*
un salón de actos	*a hall*
un comedor	*a canteen*
un campo de fútbol	*a football pitch*
un patio	*a playground*
un gimnasio	*a gym*
una piscina	*a pool*
una biblioteca	*a library*
una pista de tenis / atletismo	*a tennis court / an athletics track*
unos laboratorios	*some laboratories*
muchas aulas	*lots of classrooms*
Lo bueno / malo es que ...	*The good / bad thing is that ...*
Lo mejor / peor es que ...	*The best / worst thing is that ...*
Lo que más me gusta es / son ...	*What I like most is / are ...*
Lo que menos me gusta es / son ...	*What I like least is / are ...*
no ...ningún / ninguna	*not a single ...*
ni ... ni ...	*(n)either ...(n)or*

nada	*nothing / anything*
nadie	*no one / anyone*
tampoco	*not either*

Had a look ☐ **Nearly there** ☐ **Nailed it** ☐

Mi insti es ...	*My school is ...*
mixto / femenino / masculino	*mixed / all girls / all boys*
público / privado	*state / private*
pequeño / grande	*small / large*
moderno / antiguo	*modern / old*
En mi escuela primaria había ...	*In my primary school there was / were ...*
Mi escuela primaria tenía ...	*My primary school had ...*
más / menos ...	*more / fewer / less ...*
exámenes / deberes / alumnos	*exams / homework / pupils*
muebles / espacios verdes	*furniture / green spaces*
tiempo libre	*free time*
oportunidades / instalaciones	*opportunities / facilities*
pizarras interactivas / clases	*interactive whiteboards / lessons*
aulas de informática	*ICT rooms*
donde jugar	*somewhere to play*
poco espacio	*little space*
antes / ahora	*before / now*
El edificio / El colegio	*The building / The school*
El día escolar es / era ...	*The school day is / was ...*
(in)adecuado/a / corto/a / largo/a	*(in)adequate / short / long*
Las clases son / eran ...	*The lessons are / were ...*
Instituto de Educación Secundaria (IES)	*secondary school*

Had a look ☐ **Nearly there** ☐ **Nailed it** ☐

Las normas del insti — *School rules*

Tengo que llevar ...	*I have to wear ...*
Tenemos que llevar ...	*We have to wear ...*
(No) Llevo ...	*I (don't) wear ...*
(No) Llevamos	*We (don't) wear ...*
Es obligatorio llevar ...	*It's compulsory to wear ...*
un jersey (de punto)	*a (knitted) sweater*
un vestido	*a dress*
una camisa	*a shirt*
una camiseta	*a T-shirt*
una chaqueta (a rayas)	*a (striped) jacket*
una chaqueta de punto	*a cardigan*
una corbata	*a tie*
una falda (a cuadros)	*a (checked) skirt*
unos pantalones	*trousers*
unos calcetines	*socks*
unos zapatos	*shoes*
unos vaqueros	*jeans*
unas medias	*tights*

Had a look ☐ **Nearly there** ☐ **Nailed it** ☐

oscuro / claro	*dark / light*
a rayas / a cuadros	*striped / checked*
bonito / feo	*pretty / ugly*
cómodo / incómodo	*comfortable / uncomfortable*
anticuado / elegante / formal	*old-fashioned / smart / formal*
El uniforme ...	*Uniform ...*
mejora la disciplina	*improves discipline*
limita la individualidad	*limits individuality*
da una imagen positiva del insti	*gives a positive image of the school*
ahorra tiempo por la mañana	*saves time in the morning*

Had a look ☐ **Nearly there** ☐ **Nailed it** ☐

Está prohibido ...	*It is forbidden ...*
No se permite ...	*You are not allowed to ...*
No se debe ...	*You / One must not ...*
comer chicle	*chew chewing gum*
usar el móvil en clase	*use your phone in lessons*
dañar las instalaciones	*damage the facilities*
ser agresivo o grosero	*be agressive or rude*
correr en los pasillos	*run in the corridors*
llevar piercings	*have visible piercings*
Hay que ...	*It is necessary ...*
ser puntual	*to be on time*
respetar el turno de palabra	*to wait for your turn to speak*
mantener limpio el patio	*to keep the playground clean*
La norma más importante es ...	*the most important rule is ...*
respetar a los demás	*to respect others*

Had a look ☐ **Nearly there** ☐ **Nailed it** ☐

Las normas son ...	*The rules are ...*
necesarias / demasiado severas	*necessary / too strict*
para fomentar la buena disciplina	*for promoting good discipline*
para limitar la libertad de expresión	*for limiting freedom of expression*
para fastidiar a los alumnos	*for annoying the pupils*
sacar buenas / malas notas	*to get good / bad grades*
Estoy de acuerdo.	*I agree.*
¡Qué va!	*No way!*
¡Qué horror!	*How awful!*
¡Qué bien!	*How great!*
Un problema de mi insti es ...	*One problem in my school is ...*
el estrés de los exámenes	*exam stress*
el acoso escolar	*bullying*
la presión del grupo	*peer pressure*
Hay (unos) alumnos que ...	*There are (some) pupils who ...*
se burlan de otros	*make fun of others*

M 2

sufren intimidación	*are victims of bullying*
tienen miedo de …	*are afraid of …*
hacen novillos	*skip lessons / skive*
quieren ser parte de la pandilla	*want to be part of the friendship group*
son una mala influencia	*are a bad influence*

Had a look ☐ **Nearly there** ☐ **Nailed it** ☐

¿Cómo es tu día escolar? / *What is your school day like?*

normalmente	*usually*
Salgo de casa a las …	*I leave home at …*
Voy …	*I go …*
a pie / andando	*on foot / walking*
en bici / en autobús / en coche	*by bike / by bus / by car*
en metro / en taxi / en tren	*by underground / by taxi / by train*
Las clases empiezan / terminan a las …	*Lessons start / finish at …*
Tenemos … clases al día.	*We have … lessons per day.*
Cada clase dura … minutos.	*Each lessons lasts … minutes.*
El recreo / La hora de comer es a la(s)…	*Break / Lunch is at …*

Had a look ☐ **Nearly there** ☐ **Nailed it** ☐

¿Qué vas a hacer? / *What are you going to do?*

Voy / Vas / Vamos a …	*I'm going / You're going / We're going to …*
llegar / salir / estar	*arrive / go out / be*
ir en coche / andando	*go by car / walk*
llevar ropa de calle	*wear casual clothes / non-uniform*
ir / comer juntos	*go / eat together*
hacer una visita guiada	*do a guided tour*
ver los edificios	*see the buildings*
pasar todo el día en …	*spend the whole day in …*
asistir a clases	*attend lessons*
practicar el español	*practise Spanish*
ir de excursión	*go on a trip*
tener una programación variada	*have a varied programme*
Va a …	*It's going to …*
ser fácil / guay	*be easy / cool*

Had a look ☐ **Nearly there** ☐ **Nailed it** ☐

Las actividades extraescolares / *Extra-curricular activities*

Toco la trompeta …	*I play / I've been playing the trumpet …*
Canto en el coro …	*I sing / I've been singing in the choir …*
Voy al club de …	*I go / I've been going to the … club*
Soy miembro del club de …	*I am / I've been a member of the … club*
ajedrez / judo / teatro / periodismo	*chess / judo / drama / reporters*
lectores / Ecoescuela / fotografía	*reading / eco-schools / photography*
desde hace … años / meses	*for … years / months*

Had a look ☐ **Nearly there** ☐ **Nailed it** ☐

Para mí …	*For me …*
Pienso que / Creo que …	*I think that …*
las actividades extraescolares son …	*extra-curricular activities are …*
muy divertidas	*a lot of fun*
algo diferente / un éxito	*something different / an achievement*
te ayudan a …	*they help you to …*
olvidar las presiones del colegio	*forget the pressures of school*
desarrollar tus talentos	*develop your talents*
hacer nuevos amigos	*make new friends*
te dan …	*they give you …*
una sensación de logro	*a sense of achievement*
más confianza	*more confidence*
la oportunidad de ser creativo/a	*the opportunity to be creative*
la oportunidad de expresarte	*the opportunity to express yourself*

Had a look ☐ **Nearly there** ☐ **Nailed it** ☐

El año / trimestre / verano pasado …	*Last year / term / summer …*
participé en un evento especial	*I took part in a special event*
un concierto / un concurso / un torneo	*a concert / a competition / a tournament*
gané un trofeo	*I won a trophy*
toqué un solo	*I played a solo*
conseguimos la clasificación	*we achieved the award / designation*
como …	*as …*
tuvimos una charla	*we had a talk / presentation*
ganamos una competición nacional	*we won a national competition*
dimos un concierto	*we gave a concert*
¡Fue un éxito!	*It was a success!*
Este trimestre / El próximo trimestre …	*This term / Next term …*
voy a	*I'm going to …*
aprender a …	*learn to …*
continuar con …	*continue with …*
dejarlo	*stop doing it*
apuntarme al club de …	*sign up for the … club*
vamos a …	*we are going to …*
montar una obra de teatro	*put on a play*
conseguir	*achieve*

Had a look ☐ **Nearly there** ☐ **Nailed it** ☐

Extra words I should know for reading and listening activities

Lo que hacemos en el insti	***What we do at school***
apoyar	*to support / to back / to help*
castigar	*to punish*
conseguir	*to get / to achieve*
contestar	*to answer*
dar la bienvenida*	*to welcome*
dejar en paz	*to leave alone / in peace*
enseñar	*to teach*
entregar	*to hand in*
esforzarse	*to make an effort*
estudiar	*to study*
exigir	*to demand*
ganar	*to win*
lograr	*to achieve*
mejorar	*to improve*
memorizar	*to memorise*
pedir prestado	*to borrow*
refugiarse	*to take refuge*
restringir	*to restrict*
saber	*to know*
tocar la trompeta / el saxofón etc.**	*to play the trumpet / saxophone etc.*

Had a look ☐ **Nearly there** ☐ **Nailed it** ☐

Lo que hay en el insti	***What there is at school***
la academia	*academy / school post-16 (for certain careers)*
el apoyo	*help / support / backing*
la carpeta	*folder / file*
el castigo	*punishment*
clases intensivas de refuerzo escolar	*intensive revision classes*
clases particulares	*private lessons*
el/la compañero/a	*fellow student*
el despacho	*office*
edificios modernos / antiguos / recién renovados	*modern / old / recently renovated buildings*
la enseñanza	*teaching / education*
la ESO (Educación Secundaria Obligatoria)	*secondary education from 12 to 16 years old*
el intercambio	*exchange*
el internado	*boarding school*
la lectura	*reading*
la libertad de expresión	*freedom of expression*
el patio cubierto	*covered playground*
el polideportivo	*sports hall*
el salón de actos	*auditorium / assembly hall*

Had a look ☐ **Nearly there** ☐ **Nailed it** ☐

Expresiones y descripciones	***Expressions and descriptions***
¡No es justo!	*It isn't fair!*
¿Qué opinas de …?	*What do you think about …?*
apropiado	*appropriate*
bien equipado	*well-equipped*
el uniforme limita la individualidad	*uniform limits your individuality*
es la asignatura más exigente	*it's the most demanding subject*
los amigos cuentan más	*friends are more important*
me fastidia …	*… annoys me*
me hace pensar	*he/she/it makes me think*
me inspiró mucho	*it inspired me a lot*
mi profe me deja trabajar a mi manera	*my teacher lets me work in my own way*
mi profesor me cae bien	*I like my teacher*
nos ofrece más oportunidades	*it gives us more opportunities*
repetir los examenes	*resit exams*
superestresado/a	*highly stressed*

Had a look ☐ **Nearly there** ☐ **Nailed it** ☐

***Break unfamiliar words to work out their meaning**

If you know the meanings of component parts of unfamiliar words and phrases you can often work out what they mean. So for example the component parts of *dar la bienvenida* are:
dar to give
bien well
venida from *venir* to come

****Learn and use the right verbs**

To play an instrument in Spanish is *tocar un instrumento*. Don't fall into the trap of using the verb *jugar*.
Note too that the spelling of the 'I' form in the preterite changes.
Example: *Toqué el piano ayer.*

Words I should know for speaking and writing activities

¿Qué aplicaciones usas?	***What apps do you use?***
Uso … para …	*I use … (in order) to …*
ver mis series favoritas	*watch my favourite series*
organizar las salidas con mis amigos	*organise to go out with my friends*
controlar mi actividad física / las calorías	*monitor my physical activity / my calorie intake*
contactar con mi familia	*get in touch with my family*
chatear con mis amigos	*chat with my friends*
La tengo desde hace … meses	*I've had it for … months*
Es una aplicación buena para …	*It's a good app for …*
buscar y descargar música	*looking for and downloading music*
pasar el tiempo / el rato	*passing the time*
sacar / editar / personalizar fotos	*taking / editing / personalising photos*
compartir / subir fotos	*sharing / uploading photos*
estar en contacto	*keeping in touch*
conocer a nueva gente	*meeting new people*
subir y ver vídeos	*uploading and watching videos*
chatear y mandar mensajes	*chatting and sending messages*

Had a look ☐ **Nearly there** ☐ **Nailed it** ☐

Es / No es …	*It is / It isn't …*
una red social	*a social network*
amplio/a	*extensive*
cómodo/a	*convenient*
divertido/a	*fun*
necesario/a	*necessary*
peligroso/a	*dangerous*
práctico/a	*practical*
rápido/a	*quick*
fácil de usar	*easy to use*
popular	*popular*
útil	*useful*
gratis	*free*
un canal de comunicación	*a channel / means of communication*
una pérdida de tiempo	*a waste of time*
Soy / Es adicto/a a …	*I am / He/She is addicted to …*
Estoy / Está enganchado/a a …	*I am / He/She is hooked on …*
Lo único malo es que …	*The only bad thing is that …*
te engancha	*it gets you hooked*

Had a look ☐ **Nearly there** ☐ **Nailed it** ☐

¿Qué estás haciendo?	***What are you doing?***
Estoy …	*I am …*
actualizando mi página de Facebook	*updating my Facebook page*
editando mis fotos	*editing my photos*
Estás / Está / Están …	*You are / He/She is / They are …*
escuchando música	*listening to music*
esperando a (David)	*waiting for (David)*
descansando	*relaxing*
pensando en salir	*thinking about going out*
preparando algo para merendar	*preparing something for tea*
repasando para un examen	*revising for an exam*
tomando el sol	*sunbathing*
haciendo footing	*jogging*
haciendo el vago	*lazing about*
leyendo	*reading*
viendo una peli	*watching a film*
escribiendo	*writing*

Had a look ☐ **Nearly there** ☐ **Nailed it** ☐

¿Quieres salir conmigo?	*Do you want to go out with me?*
No puedo porque …	*I can't because …*
está lloviendo	*it's raining*
tengo que …	*I have to …*
salir	*go out*
visitar a (mi abuela)	*visit (my grandmother)*
cuidar a (mi hermano)	*look after (my brother)*
hacer los deberes	*do homework*
quiero …	*I want …*
subir mis fotos a …	*to upload my photos to …*
quedarme en casa	*to stay at home*
¡Qué rollo!	*What a pain!*
¿A qué hora quedamos?	*What time shall we meet?*
¿Dónde quedamos?	*Where shall we meet?*
en la Plaza Mayor	*in the main square*
debajo de	*underneath*
detrás de	*behind*
delante de	*in front of*
enfrente de	*opposite*
al lado de	*next to*

Had a look ☐ **Nearly there** ☐ **Nailed it** ☐

¿Qué te gusta leer?	***What do you like reading?***
los blogs	*blogs*
los tebeos / los cómics	*comics*
los periódicos	*newspapers*
las revistas	*magazines*
las poesías	*poems*
las novelas de ciencia ficción	*science fiction novels*

las novelas de amor	*romantic novels*
las historias de vampiros	*vampire stories*
las biografías	*biographies*

Had a look ☐ **Nearly there** ☐ **Nailed it** ☐

¿Con qué frecuencia lees?	***How often do you read?***
cada día / todos los días	*every day*
a menudo	*often*
generalmente	*generally*
de vez en cuando	*from time to time*
una vez a la semana	*once a week*
dos veces al mes	*twice a month*
una vez al año	*once a year*
nunca	*never*

Had a look ☐ **Nearly there** ☐ **Nailed it** ☐

¿Qué es mejor, leer en papel o en la red?	***What's better, reading paper books or online?***
Leer en formato digital …	*Reading in digital format …*
protege el planeta	*protects the planet*
no malgasta papel	*doesn't waste paper*
cansa la vista	*tires your eyes*
depende de la energía eléctrica	*relies on electricity*
te permite llevar contigo miles de libros	*allows you to take thousands of books with you*
cuesta mucho menos	*costs a lot less*
fastidia porque no hay numeración de páginas	*is annoying because there is no page numbering*
Los libros electrónicos / Los e-books …	*Electronic books / E-books …*
son fáciles de transportar	*are easy to transport*
son más ecológicos / baratos	*are more environmentally friendly / cheaper*
no ocupan espacio	*don't take up space*

Had a look ☐ **Nearly there** ☐ **Nailed it** ☐

Una desventaja es …	*One disadvantage is …*
el uso de batería	*the battery use*
Me gusta / Prefiero …	*I like / I prefer …*
tocar las páginas	*to touch the pages*
pasar las páginas a mano	*to turn the pages by hand*
escribir anotaciones	*to write notes*
leer horas y horas	*to read for hours and hours*
un ratón de biblioteca	*a bookworm*
un fan del manga	*a manga fan*
un libro tradicional	*a traditional book*
un libro de verdad	*a real book*

Had a look ☐ **Nearly there** ☐ **Nailed it** ☐

La familia	***Family***
el padre / la madre	*father / mother*
el padrastro / la madrastra	*step-father / step-mother*
el hermano / la hermana	*brother / sister*
el hermanastro / la hermanastra	*step-brother / step-sister*
el abuelo / la abuela	*grandfather / grandmother*
el bisabuelo / la bisabuela	*great grandfather / great grandmother*
el tío / la tía	*uncle / aunt*
el primo / la prima	*male cousin / female cousin*
el sobrino / la sobrina	*nephew / niece*
el marido / la mujer	*husband / wife*
el hijo / la hija	*son / daughter*
el nieto / la nieta	*grandson / granddaughter*
mayor / menor	*older / younger*

Had a look ☐ **Nearly there** ☐ **Nailed it** ☐

¿Cómo es?	***What is he/she like?***
Tiene los ojos …	*He/She has … eyes*
azules / verdes / marrones / grises	*blue / green / brown / grey*
grandes / pequeños / brillantes	*big / small / bright*
Tiene el pelo …	*He/She has … hair*
moreno / rubio / castaño / rojo	*dark brown / blond / mid-brown / red*
corto / largo	*short / long*
rizado / liso / ondulado	*curly / straight / wavy*
fino / de punta	*fine / spiky*

Had a look ☐ **Nearly there** ☐ **Nailed it** ☐

Tiene …	*He/She has …*
la piel blanca / morena	*fair / dark skin*
la cara redonda / alargada	*a round / oval face*
los dientes prominentes	*big teeth*
pecas	*freckles*
Lleva …	*He/She wears / has …*
gafas	*glasses*
barba	*a beard*
bigote	*a moustache*
Es …	*He/She is …*
alto/a / bajo/a	*tall / short*
delgado/a / gordito/a / gordo/a	*slim / chubby / fat*
calvo/a	*bald*
moreno/a	*dark-haired*
rubio/a	*fair-haired*
castaño/a	*brown-haired*
pelirrojo/a	*a redhead*
español / española	*Spanish*
inglés / inglesa	*English*
peruano / peruana	*Peruvian*

M 3

M 3

Mide 1, 60.	*He/She is 1m60 tall.*
No es ni alto ni bajo.	*He/She is neither tall nor short.*
(No) Nos parecemos físicamente.	*We (don't) look like each other.*

Had a look ☐ **Nearly there** ☐ **Nailed it** ☐

¿Cómo es de carácter?	***What is he/she like as a person?***
Como persona, es …	*As a person, he/she is …*
optimista / pesimista	*optimistic / pessimistic*
simpático/a / antipático/a	*nice / nasty*
trabajador(a) / perezoso/a	*hard-working / lazy*
generoso/a / tacaño/a	*generous / mean*
hablador(a) / callado/a	*chatty / quiet*
divertido/a / gracioso/a / serio/a	*fun / funny / serious*
fiel / infiel	*loyal / disloyal*
feliz / triste	*happy / sad*
ordenado/a / caótico/a	*tidy / chaotic*
enérgico/a / animado/a / tranquilo/a	*energetic / lively / calm*
pensativo/a	*thoughtful*
comprensivo/a	*understanding*
honesto/a	*honest*
alegre	*cheerful*
molesto/a	*annoying*
ambicioso/a	*ambitious*
egoísta	*selfish*
Está feliz / triste.	*He/She is happy / sad.*

Had a look ☐ **Nearly there** ☐ **Nailed it** ☐

¿Te llevas bien con tu familia?	***Do you get on well with your family?***
(No) Me llevo bien con … porque …	*I (don't) get on well with … because …*
me apoya	*he/she supports me*
me acepta como soy	*he/she accepts me as I am*
nunca me critica	*he/she never criticises me*
tenemos mucho en común	*we have a lot in common*
Me divierto con …	*I have a good time with …*
Me peleo con …	*I argue with …*
Nos llevamos superbién.	*We get on really well.*
Nos llevamos como el perro y el gato.	*We fight like cat and dog.*
Nos divertimos siempre.	*We always have a good time.*

Had a look ☐ **Nearly there** ☐ **Nailed it** ☐

¿Cómo es un buen amigo / una buena amiga?	***What is a good friend like?***
Un buen amigo es alguien que …	*A good friend is someone who …*
te apoya	*supports you*
te escucha	*listens to you*
te conoce bien	*knows you well*
te acepta como eres	*accepts you as you are*
te quiere mucho	*likes / loves you a lot*
te da consejos	*gives you advice*
te hace reír	*makes you laugh*
no te critica	*doesn't criticise you*
nunca te juzga	*never judges you*
Conocí a mi mejor amigo/a …	*I met my best friend …*
Nos conocimos	*We met / got to know each other*
Nos hicimos amigos	*We became friends*
Nos hicimos novios	*We started going out*
convivimos	*we lived together*
nos casamos	*we got married*
Es el amor de mi vida.	*He/She is the love of my life.*
Tenemos … en común.	*We have … in common.*
nos gustan (las mismas cosas)	*we like (the same things)*
nos encantan (las películas)	*we love (films)*

Had a look ☐ **Nearly there** ☐ **Nailed it** ☐

Extra words I should know for reading and listening activities

Describiendo a una persona	***Describing someone***
atrevido/a	*cheeky / insolent / bold / daring*
celoso/a	*jealous*
cómico/a	*comical*
cuidadoso/a	*careful*
dinámico/a	*dynamic*
educado/a*	*polite*
Es tan tranquilo/a como el agua de un pozo.**	*(lit.) He/She is as calm as water in a well.*
explosivo/a	*explosive*
histérico/a	*hysterical*
idealista	*idealistic*
modesto/a	*modest*
no se impacienta nunca con nadie	*he/she never loses his/her patience with anyone*
No se pelea nunca.	*He/She doesn't ever argue.*
paciente	*patient*
romántico/a	*romantic*
seguro/a de sí mismo	*self-assured*
sincero/a	*sincere*
sus ojos son tan pequeños como dos botones / grandes / redondos	*his/her eyes are as small as two big / round buttons*
tiene el pelo negro como el carbón	*her hair is as black as coal*
tímido/a	*shy*
travieso/a	*naughty*

Had a look ☐ **Nearly there** ☐ **Nailed it** ☐

Relacionándose con la gente	***Relating to people***
aconsejar	*to advise*
acordar	*to agree on*
aguantar	*to bear / to put up with*
agradecer	*to thank / to be grateful for*
asentir	*to nod*
celebrar	*to celebrate*
chatear	*to chat / to talk*
confiar	*to trust*
corroborar	*to agree / to corroborate*
despedir(se)	*to say goodbye*
disculpar(se)	*to apologise*
hacer multitarea	*to multitask*
llorar	*to cry*
ocuparse de	*to look after*
parecerse a	*to look like*
recargar	*to recharge*
relacionarse con	*to make contact with / to get on with (people)*
(no) tener mucho en común	*(not) to have much in common*
tratar (de / con)	*to treat each other / to have dealings with*

Had a look ☐ **Nearly there** ☐ **Nailed it** ☐

Relaciones de pareja	***Partnerships***
el anillo	*ring*
la boda	*wedding*
comprometerse	*to get engaged*
el compromiso	*engagement / commitment*
el esposo	*husband / spouse*
el estado civil	*marital status*
el matrimonio	*marriage*
la pareja	*couple / partner*
separarse	*to separate / to split up*
el/la viudo/a	*widower/widow*

Had a look ☐ **Nearly there** ☐ **Nailed it** ☐

M 3

***Watch out for false friends**

When you describe someone as being *educado* in Spanish, for example *Mi padre es muy educado,* you are not talking about your father's education, you are saying that your father is very 'polite'. If you wanted to say that someone is 'rude' or 'impolite' you would use *maleducado.*

****Don't always try to translate word for word**

The literal translation of *Es tan tranquilo como el agua de un pozo* doesn't sound very good in English although it is useful to note that *pozo* means 'well'. When this happens, try to find an equivalent phrase. You could for example translate the Spanish simile with another simile in English, for example 'She is as cool as a cucumber.'

Words I should know for speaking and writing activities

La paga	***Pocket money***
Mis padres me dan …	*My parents give me …*
Mi madre / padre me da …	*My mum / dad gives me …*
…euros a la semana / al mes	*…euros a week / a month*
Gasto mi paga en …	*I spend my pocket money on …*
También compro …	*I also buy …*
saldo para el móvil	*credit for my phone*
ropa / joyas / maquillaje	*clothes / jewellery / make-up*
zapatillas de marca	*designer trainers*
videojuegos / revistas	*computer games / magazines*

Had a look ☐ **Nearly there** ☐ **Nailed it** ☐

Mis ratos libres	***My free time***
las actividades de ocio	*leisure activities*
Tengo muchos pasatiempos.	*I have lots of hobbies.*
A la hora de comer …	*At lunchtime …*
Cuando tengo tiempo …	*When I have time …*
Después del insti …	*After school …*
Los fines de semana …	*At weekends …*
Mientras desayuno / como …	*Whilst I have breakfast / lunch …*
juego al billar / futbolín	*I play billiards / table football*
monto en bici / monopatín	*I ride my bike / I skateboard*
quedo con mis amigos	*I meet up with friends*
voy de compras	*I go shopping*
mi pasión es la música / la lectura	*my passion is music / reading*

Had a look ☐ **Nearly there** ☐ **Nailed it** ☐

Suelo …	*I tend to / I usually …*
descansar	*rest*
escuchar música / la radio	*listen to music / the radio*
hacer deporte	*do sport*
ir al cine	*go to the cinema*
leer libros / revistas / periódicos	*read books / magazines / newspapers*
salir con amigos	*go out with friends*
usar el ordenador	*use the computer*
ver la tele	*watch TV*
Es divertido / relajante / sano	*It's fun / relaxing / healthy*
Soy creativo/a / perezoso/a / sociable	*I'm creative / lazy / sociable*
Soy adicto/a a …	*I'm addicted to …*
me ayuda a relajarme	*it helps me to relax*
me ayuda a olvidarme de todo	*it helps me to forget everything*
me hace reír	*it makes me laugh*
necesito comunicarme / relacionarme con otra gente	*I need to have contact with other people*

Had a look ☐ **Nearly there** ☐ **Nailed it** ☐

La música	***Music***
Me gusta el soul / el rap / el dance / el hip-hop / el pop / el rock / el jazz / la música clásica / electrónica	*I like soul / rap / dance / hip-hop / pop / rock / jazz / classical / electronic music*
asistir a un concierto	*to attend a concert*
cantar (una canción)	*to sing (a song)*
tocar el teclado / el piano / la batería / la flauta / la guitarra / la trompeta	*to play the keyboard / the piano / the drums / the flute / the guitar / the trumpet*
mi cantante preferido/a es …	*my favourite singer is …*
un espectáculo	*a show*
una gira (mundial)	*a (world) tour*

Had a look ☐ **Nearly there** ☐ **Nailed it** ☐

El deporte	***Sport***
Soy / Era …	*I am / I used to be …*
(bastante / muy) deportista	*(quite / very) sporty*
miembro de un club / un equipo	*a member of a club / a team*
aficionado/a / hincha de …	*a fan of …*
un(a) fanático/a de …	*a … fanatic*
juego al …	*I play …*
jugué …	*I played …*
jugaba al …	*I used to play …*
bádminton / baloncesto	*badminton / basketball*
béisbol / balonmano	*baseball / handball*
críquet / fútbol	*cricket / football*
hockey / ping-pong	*hockey / table tennis*
rugby / tenis / voleibol	*rugby / tennis / volleyball*

Had a look ☐ **Nearly there** ☐ **Nailed it** ☐

hago …	*I do …*
hice …	*I did …*
hacía …	*I used to do …*
baile / boxeo / ciclismo	*dancing / boxing / cycling*
deportes acuáticos	*water sports*
equitación / escalada	*horseriding / climbing*
gimnasia / judo	*gymnastics / judo*
kárate / natación	*karate / swimming*
patinaje sobre hielo	*ice skating*
piragüismo / remo	*canoeing / rowing*
submarinismo	*diving*
tiro con arco	*archery*
voy …	*I go …*

fui …	*I went …*
iba …	*I used to go …*
a clases de …	*to … classes*
de pesca	*fishing*

Had a look ☐ **Nearly there** ☐ **Nailed it** ☐

ya no (juego) …	*(I) no longer (play) …*
todavía (hago) …	*(I) still (do) …*
batir un récord	*to break a record*
correr	*to run*
entrenar	*to train*
jugar un partido	*to play a match*
contra …	*against …*
marcar un gol	*to score a goal*
montar a caballo	*to go horseriding*
participar en un torneo	*to participate in a tournament*
patinar	*to skate*
Mi jugador(a) preferido/a es …	*My favourite player is …*
Su punto culminante fue cuando …	*The highlight (of his/her career) was when …*
el campeón / la campeona	*the champion*
la temporada	*the season*

Had a look ☐ **Nearly there** ☐ **Nailed it** ☐

La tele	***TV***
(No) Soy teleadicto/a.	*I'm (not) a TV addict.*
Mi programa favorito es …	*My favourite programme is …*
un concurso	*a game / quiz show*
un programa de deportes	*a sports programme*
un reality	*a reality TV show*
un documental	*a documentary*
un culebrón / una telenovela	*a soap*
una comedia	*a comedy*
una serie policíaca	*a crime series*
el telediario / las noticias	*the news*
Me gustan las comedias.	*I like comedies.*
Es / Son …	*It is / They are …*
aburrido/a/os/as	*boring*
adictivo/a/os/as	*addictive*
divertido/a/os/as	*fun*
entretenido/a/os/as	*entertaining*
tonto/a/os/as	*silly*
informativo/a/os/as	*informative*
malo/a/os/as	*bad*
emocionante(s)	*exciting*
interesante(s)	*interesting*

Had a look ☐ **Nearly there** ☐ **Nailed it** ☐

Las películas	***Films***
un misterio	*a mystery*
una película de amor	*a love film*
una película de terror	*a horror film*
una película de acción	*an action film*
una película de aventuras	*an adventure film*
una película de animación	*an animated film*
una película de ciencia ficción	*a sci-fi film*
una película de fantasía	*a fantasy film*
una película extranjera	*a foreign film*

Had a look ☐ **Nearly there** ☐ **Nailed it** ☐

Nacionalidades	***Nationalities***
americano/a	*American*
argentino/a	*Argentinian*
británico/a	*British*
chino/a	*Chinese*
griego/a	*Greek*
italiano/a	*Italian*
mexicano/a	*Mexican*
sueco/a	*Swedish*
alemán/alemana	*German*
danés/danesa	*Danish*
español(a)	*Spanish*
francés/francesa	*French*
holandés/holandesa	*Dutch*
inglés/inglesa	*English*
irlandés/irlandesa	*Irish*
japonés/japonesa	*Japanese*

Had a look ☐ **Nearly there** ☐ **Nailed it** ☐

Temas del momento	***Trending topics***
he compartido …	*I have shared …*
he comprado …	*I have bought …*
he jugado …	*I have played …*
he leído …	*I have read …*
he oído …	*I have heard …*
he roto …	*I have broken …*
he subido …	*I have uploaded …*
¿Has probado …?	*Have you tried …?*
mi hermano ha descargado …	*my brother has downloaded …*
se ha estrenado …	*… has been released.*
la nueva canción	*the new song*
el último libro	*the latest book*

Had a look ☐ **Nearly there** ☐ **Nailed it** ☐

Ya lo/la/los/las he visto.	*I have already seen it/them.*
No lo/la/los/las he visto todavía.	*I haven't seen it/them yet.*
acabo de ver / jugar a …	*I have just seen / played …*
cuenta la historia de …	*it tells the story of …*
trata de …	*it's about …*
combina el misterio con la acción	*it combines mystery with action*
el argumento es fuerte / débil	*the plot is strong / weak*
la banda sonora es buena / mala	*the soundtrack is good / bad*
los actores …	*the actors …*

M 4

los efectos especiales …	*the special effects …*
los gráficos …	*the graphics …*
los personajes …	*the characters …*
las animaciones …	*the animations …*
las canciones …	*the songs …*
son guapos/as / guay	*are good looking / cool*
son estupendos/as / impresionantes	*are great / impressive*
son originales / repetitivos/as	*are original / repetitive*

Had a look ☐ **Nearly there** ☐ **Nailed it** ☐

Ir al cine, al teatro, etc. — *Going to the cinema, theatre, etc.*

¿Qué vamos a hacer …	*What are we going to do …*
esta tarde?	*this afternoon / evening?*
esta noche?	*tonight?*
mañana / el viernes?	*tomorrow / on Friday?*
¿Tienes ganas de ir …	*Do you fancy going …*
a un concierto / un festival?	*to a concert / a festival?*
a un espectáculo de baile?	*to a dance show?*
al cine / al teatro / al circo?	*to the cinema / theatre / circus?*
¿Qué ponen?	*What's on?*
Es una película / obra de …	*It's a … film / play*
¿A qué hora empieza / termina?	*What time does it start / finish?*
Empieza / Termina a las …	*It starts / finishes at …*
Dos entradas para … / por favor para la sesión de las …	*Two tickets for … / please for the … showing / performance*
No quedan entradas.	*There are no tickets left.*
¿Hay un descuento para estudiantes?	*Is there a discount for students?*
Aquí tiene mi carné de estudiante.	*Here is my student card.*

Had a look ☐ **Nearly there** ☐ **Nailed it** ☐

¿En el cine o en casa? — *At the cinema or at home?*

(No) Me gusta ir al cine porque …	*I (don't) like going to the cinema because …*
Prefiero ver las pelis en casa porque …	*I prefer watching films at home because …*
el ambiente es mejor	*the atmosphere is better*
hay demasiadas personas	*there are too many people*
la imagen es mejor en la gran pantalla	*the picture is better on the big screen*
las entradas son muy caras	*the tickets are very expensive*
las palomitas están ricas	*the popcorn is tasty*
los asientos no son cómodos	*the seats aren't comfortable*
los otros espectadores me molestan	*the other spectators annoy me*
ponen tráilers para las nuevas pelis	*they show trailers for the new films*
si vas al baño te pierdes una parte	*if you go to the toilet you miss part of it*
tienes que hacer cola	*you have to queue*
una corrida de toros	*a bull fight*
en directo	*live*

Had a look ☐ **Nearly there** ☐ **Nailed it** ☐

Los modelos a seguir — *Role models*

Admiro a …	*I admire …*
Mi inspiración / ídolo es …	*My inspiration / idol is …*
…es un buen / mal modelo a seguir	*… is a good / bad role model*
Un buen modelo a seguir es alguien que …	*A good role model is someone who …*
apoya a organizaciones benéficas	*supports charities*
recauda fondos para …	*raises money for …*
tiene mucho talento / éxito	*is very talented / successful*
trabaja en defensa de los animales	*works in defence of animals*
usa su fama para ayudar a los demás	*uses his / her fame to help others*
se emborrachan	*they get drunk*
se comportan mal	*they behave badly*
se meten en problemas con la policía	*they get into problems with the police*

Had a look ☐ **Nearly there** ☐ **Nailed it** ☐

es amable / cariñoso/a / fuerte	*he/she is nice / affectionate / strong*
lucha por / contra …	*he/she fights for / against …*
la pobreza / la homofobia	*poverty / homophobia*
los derechos de la mujer	*women's rights*
los derechos de los refugiados	*the rights of refugees*
los niños desfavorecidos	*underprivileged children*
la justicia social	*social justice*
a pesar de sus problemas …	*despite his/her problems …*
ha batido varios récords	*he/she has broken several records*
ha creado …	*he/she has created …*
ha ganado … medallas / premios	*he/she has won … medals / awards*
ha sufrido varias enfermedades	*he/she has suffered several illnesses*
ha superado sus problemas	*he/she has overcome his/her problems*
ha tenido mucho éxito como …	*he/she has had lots of success as …*
siempre sonríe	*he/she always smiles*
solo piensa en los demás	*he/she only thinks of other people*

Had a look ☐ **Nearly there** ☐ **Nailed it** ☐

Extra words I should know for reading and listening activities

Verbos útiles	***Useful verbs***
acoger a (niños)	*to take in (children)*
aplaudir	*to clap*
combatir la injusticia	*to fight injustice*
disfrutar	*to enjoy*
entrar en el escenario	*to come on stage*
escaparse de casa	*to run away from home*
estrenarse	*to be released*
ganar* (dinero)	*to earn (money)*
gritar	*to shout*
jugar al pádel**	*to play padel tennis (kind of racquet game that started in Mexico)*
poner en escena	*to stage*
recibir	*to get / to receive*
recorrer	*to cover (distance)*
salir al mercado	*to come out on the market*
sobrevivir	*to survive*
sonreír	*to smile*
superar	*to overcome*
tener éxito	*to be successful*
vivir en las calles	*to live on the streets*

Had a look ☐ **Nearly there** ☐ **Nailed it** ☐

Expresiones y adjetivos	***Expressions and adjectives***
¡Es un crack!	*He's a real champion.*
de todos los géneros	*of all kinds*
decepcionante	*disappointing*
disponible	*available*
El deporte es mi vida.	*Sport means everything to me.*
en versión original	*undubbed / original version*
enganchado/a	*hooked*
hilarante	*hilarious*
Las canciones eran pegadizas.	*The songs were catchy.*
Me ayuda a desconectar / olvidarme de todo.	*It helps me to disconnect / forget about everything else.*
¡Qué ilusión!	*How exciting!*
¡Qué timo!	*What a rip-off!*
Soy un/a adicto/a a la adrenalina.	*I get a rush from adrenaline.*
Tiene una voz hermosa.	*He/She has a lovely voice / sings beautifully.*
valiente	*brave*

Had a look ☐ **Nearly there** ☐ **Nailed it** ☐

Nombres útiles	***Useful nouns***
el argumento	*plot*
la carrera profesional	*professional career*
el comportamiento	*behaviour*
el/la delantero/a	*forward (sport)*
el ejemplar	*copy (of a book)*
un/a embajador(a) de buena voluntad	*a goodwill ambassador*
el equipo de fútbol femenino	*women's football team*
el estilo libre	*crawl / free style (swimming)*
el estilo mariposa	*butterfly stroke (swimming)*
la estrella	*star / champion (in sport)*
el estreno	*release (of a film / record etc.)*
el/la ganador(a)	*winner*
el/la goleador(a)	*scorer*
el héroe anónimo	*unsung hero*
el/la jugador(a)	*player*
la lesión	*injury*
una noche inolvidable	*a night to remember*
la resistencia física y mental	*physical and mental stamina*
la taquilla	*ticket office*
el título mundial	*world record*

Had a look ☐ **Nearly there** ☐ **Nailed it** ☐

M
4

***Use context to work out translations of words with more than one meaning**

The verb *ganar* can mean 'to earn', 'to win' or 'to gain'. When you are reading or listening, work out the correct meaning from the context. Look at the sentences below and work out the different meanings:

*Para **ganar** dinero, normalmente ayudo a mis padres con algunas tareas en casa.*

*En julio cantamos en un concurso nacional y lo **ganamos**.*

***Ganará** mucha experiencia trabajando como voluntario.*

****Learn irregular verb forms and spelling changes**

Remember that *jugar* is one of the verbs in which the spelling changes for the 'I' form of the preterite, for example, *Juego al fútbol todos los días.* → *Jugué al fútbol ayer.*

Words I should know for speaking and writing activities

En mi ciudad	***In my town***
Hay … / Mi ciudad tiene …	*There is/are … / My town has …*
un ayuntamiento	*a town hall*
un bar / muchos bares	*a bar / lots of bars*
un castillo (en ruinas)	*a (ruined) castle*
un cine	*a cinema*
un mercado	*a market*
un museo / unos museos	*a museum / a few museums*
un parque	*a park*
un polideportivo	*a sports centre*
un puerto	*a port*
muchos restaurantes	*lots of restaurants*
un teatro	*a theatre*
una biblioteca	*a library*
una bolera	*a bowling alley*
una iglesia	*a church*
una piscina	*a swimming pool*
una playa / unas playas	*a beach / some beaches*
una Plaza Mayor	*a town square*
una pista de hielo	*an ice rink*
una oficina de Correos	*a post office*
una tienda / muchas tiendas	*a shop / lots of shops*
muchos lugares de interés	*lots of sights*
algo / mucho que hacer	*something / a lot to do*
no hay nada que hacer	*there is nothing to do*

Had a look ☐ **Nearly there** ☐ **Nailed it** ☐

Vivo en un pueblo …	*I live in a … village*
histórico / moderno	*historic / modern*
tranquilo / ruidoso	*quiet / noisy*
turístico / industrial	*touristy / industrial*
bonito / feo	*pretty / ugly*
Está situado/a en … del país.	*It is situated in … of the country.*
el norte / el sur el este / el oeste	*the north / the south / the east / the west*

Had a look ☐ **Nearly there** ☐ **Nailed it** ☐

¿Por dónde se va al / a la …?	***How do you get to the …?***
¿Dónde está el / la …?	*Where is the …?*
¿El / La … está cerca / lejos de aquí?	*Is the … nearby / far away from here?*
sigue todo recto	*go straight on*
gira a la derecha / izquierda	*turn right / left*
toma la primera / segunda / tercera calle a la derecha / a la izquierda	*take the first / second / third road on the right / left*
pasa el puente / los semáforos	*go over the bridge / the traffic lights*
cruza la plaza / la calle	*cross the square / the street*
coge el autobús número 37	*take the number 37 bus*
está …	*it is …*
en la esquina / al final de la calle	*on the corner / at the end of the street*
al lado del museo	*next to the museum*
enfrente de …	*opposite …*

Had a look ☐ **Nearly there** ☐ **Nailed it** ☐

¿Cómo es tu zona?	***What is your area like?***
está situado/a en un valle	*it is situated in a valley*
entre el desierto y la sierra	*between the desert and the mountains*
al lado del río / mar Mediterráneo	*by the river / Mediterranean sea*
Está …	*It is …*
rodeado/a de volcanes / sierra	*surrounded by volcanoes / mountains*
lleno/a de bosques / selvas	*full of woods / forests*
a … metros sobre el nivel del mar	*at … metres above the sea level*
Tiene …	*It has …*
unos impresionantes paisajes naturales	*some amazing natural landscapes*
varias influencias culturales	*various cultural influences*
el bullicio de la ciudad	*the hustle and bustle of a city*
El clima es …	*The climate is …*
soleado / caluroso / seco / templado / frío	*sunny / hot / dry / mild / cold*
llueve (muy) poco / a menudo	*it rains (very) little / often*
en primavera / verano / otoño / invierno	*in spring / summer / autumn / winter*
hay mucha marcha	*there is lots going on*

Had a look ☐ **Nearly there** ☐ **Nailed it** ☐

Es …	*It is …*
mi ciudad natal / mi lugar favorito	*my home town / my favourite place*
acogedor/a / atractivo/a	*welcoming / attractive*
famoso/a / conocido/a por	*famous for / well-known for*
una región muy húmeda	*a very humid region*
una zona muy montañosa / pintoresca	*a mountainous / picturesque area*
tan fácil desplazarse	*so easy to get around*
Se puede …	*You / One can …*
estar mucho tiempo al aire libre	*spend lots of time in the open air*
subir a la torre	*go up the tower*
hacer un recorrido en autobús	*do a bus tour*
disfrutar de las vistas / del ambiente	*enjoy the views / the atmosphere*

viajar en el AVE	*travel on the AVE high-speed train*
pasear por los lagos artificiales	*go boating on the artificial lakes*
apreciar la arquitectura variada	*appreciate the variety of architecture*
aprovechar el buen tiempo	*make the most of the good weather*
Se pueden …	*You / One can …*
probar platos típicos	*try local dishes*
practicar deportes acuáticos	*do water sports*
ver edificios de estilos muy diferentes	*see buildings with very different styles*
alquilar bolas de agua	*hire water balls*
practicar senderismo y ciclismo	*go hiking / trekking and cycling*

Had a look ☐ **Nearly there** ☐ **Nailed it** ☐

En la oficina de turismo	***At the tourist office***
¿Me puede dar …?	*Can you give me …?*
un plano de la ciudad	*a map of the town / city*
más información sobre …	*more information about …*
¿Cuánto cuesta una entrada?	*How much is a ticket?*
para adultos / niños	*for adults / children*
¿Dónde se pueden sacar las entradas?	*Where can you get tickets?*
¿A qué hora …?	*What time …?*
sale el autobús?	*does the bus leave?*
abre …?	*does …open?*
¿Hay visitas guiadas?	*Are there guided tours?*
¿Me puede recomendar …?	*Can you recommend …?*
un restaurante típico	*a typical restaurant*
un hotel / una excursión	*a hotel / a trip*

Had a look ☐ **Nearly there** ☐ **Nailed it** ☐

¿Qué haremos mañana?	***What will we do tomorrow?***
Sacaré muchas fotos.	*I will take lots of photos.*
Subiremos al teleférico.	*We will go up on the cable car.*
Bajaremos a pie.	*We will go down on foot.*
Pasaremos entre las nubes.	*We will go through the clouds.*
Iremos a la playa / a la montaña / de excursión en barco.	*We will go to the beach / to the mountains / on a boat trip.*
Haremos piragüismo.	*We will go canoeing.*
Podremos hacer paddlesurf.	*We will be able to go paddlesurfing.*
Podrás comprar regalos.	*You will be able to buy presents.*
será genial / mejor	*it will be great / better*
nos llevará	*he/she will take us*
Estoy (muy) a gusto.	*I am feeling (very much) at home.*
¡Buena idea!	*Good idea!*
De acuerdo.	*OK.*
¡Qué pena! / ¡Qué mal (rollo)!	*What a shame! / What a nightmare!*
¡Qué triste!	*How sad!*

Had a look ☐ **Nearly there** ☐ **Nailed it** ☐

¿Qué tiempo hará?	***What will be weather be like?***
Hará sol / viento.	*It will be sunny / windy.*
Habrá …	*There will be …*
nubes / claros / chubascos	*clouds / clear spells / showers*
una ola de calor	*a heat wave*
truenos y relámpagos	*thunder and lightning*
temperaturas más altas / bajas	*higher / lower temperatures*
granizo / brisas fuertes	*hail / strong winds*
periodos soleados	*sunny spells*
lloverá (bastante)	*it will rain (quite a bit)*
Las temperaturas subirán / bajarán.	*The temperatures will rise / fall.*
El tiempo …	*The weather …*
será variable	*will be variable*
se despejará	*will clear up*
cambiará	*will change*
no nos importará	*will not matter to us*

Had a look ☐ **Nearly there** ☐ **Nailed it** ☐

Las tiendas	***Shops***
el banco	*bank*
el estanco	*tobacconist's*
la cafetería	*café*
la carnicería	*butcher's*
la estación de trenes	*train station*
la farmacia	*pharmacy / chemist*
la frutería	*greengrocer's*
la joyería	*jeweller's*
la librería	*book shop*
la panadería	*bakery*
la papelería	*stationery shop*
la pastelería	*cake shop*
la peluquería	*hairdresser's*
la pescadería	*fish shop*
la tienda de ropa	*clothes shop*
la zapatería	*shoe shop*

Had a look ☐ **Nearly there** ☐ **Nailed it** ☐

un regalo	*a present*
sellos	*stamps*
una carta / unas cartas	*a letter / a few letters*
recoger	*to pick up*
mandar	*to send*
horario comercial / horas de apertura	*business hours / opening hours*
de lunes a viernes	*from Monday to Friday*

abre a la(s) … / cierra a la(s) …	*it opens at … / it closes at …*
no cierra a mediodía	*it doesn't close at midday*
cerrado domingos y festivos	*closed on Sundays and public holidays*
abierto todos los días	*open every day*

Had a look ☐ **Nearly there** ☐ **Nailed it** ☐

Recuerdos y regalos	***Souvenirs and presents***
el abanico	*fan*
el chorizo	*chorizo (sausage)*
el llavero	*key ring*
el oso de peluche	*teddy bear*
los pendientes	*earrings*
la gorra	*cap*
la taza	*mug*
las golosinas	*sweets*
las pegatinas	*stickers*
¿Me puede ayudar?	*Can you help me?*
Quiero comprar …	*I want to buy …*
¿Tiene uno/a/os/as más barato/a/os/as?	*Do you have a cheaper one / cheaper ones?*
un billete de (cincuenta) euros	*a (fifty) euro note*
Tengo cambio.	*I have change.*

Had a look ☐ **Nearly there** ☐ **Nailed it** ☐

Quejas	***Complaints***
Quiero devolver …	*I want to return …*
está roto/a	*it is broken*
es demasiado estrecho/a / largo/a	*it is too tight / long*
tiene un agujero / una mancha	*it has a hole / a stain*
falta un botón	*it's missing a button*
¿Puede reembolsarme (el dinero)?	*Can you reimburse me (the money)?*
Podemos hacer un cambio.	*We can exchange (it).*
¿Qué me recomienda?	*What do you recommend?*
¿Qué tal …? / ¿Qué te parece(n) …?	*What about …? / What do you think of …?*
Te queda bien.	*It suits you.*
Te quedan demasiado grandes.	*They are too big for you.*
una talla más grande / pequeña	*a bigger / smaller size*
en rebajas	*on sale*
Me lo/la/los/las llevo.	*I'll take it / them.*

Had a look ☐ **Nearly there** ☐ **Nailed it** ☐

De compras	***Shopping***
Normalmente voy … / Suelo ir …	*Usually I go … / I tend to go …*
a los centros comerciales	*to shopping centres*
de tiendas con mis amigos	*shopping with my friends*
Nunca me ha gustado / Prefiero / Odio …	*I've never liked / I prefer / I hate …*
comprar en …	*shopping in …*
cadenas / grandes almacenes	*chain stores / department stores*
tiendas de diseño / segunda mano	*designer shops / second-hand shops*
comprar por Internet / en la red	*shopping on the internet / online*
hacer cola	*queueing*
porque …	*because …*
es más económico / práctico / cómodo	*it's cheaper / more practical / more convenient*
es un buen sitio para pasar la tarde	*it's a good place for spending the afternoon*
hay más variedad / demasiada gente	*there is more variety / there are too many people*
los precios son más bajos	*the prices are lower*
hay más ofertas	*there are more offers*
ropa alternativa / de moda	*alternative clothing / fashionable clothing*
gangas	*bargains*
artículos de marca	*branded items*

Had a look ☐ **Nearly there** ☐ **Nailed it** ☐

Los pros y los contras de la ciudad	***The for and against of living in a city***
Lo mejor de vivir en la ciudad es que …	*The best thing about living in a city is that …*
es tan fácil desplazarse	*it's so easy to get around*
hay una red de transporte público	*there is a public transport system*
hay tantas diversiones	*there are so many things to do*
hay muchas posibilidades de trabajo	*there are lots of job opportunities*
Lo peor es que …	*The worst thing is that …*
el centro es tan ruidoso	*the centre is so noisy*
hay tanto tráfico / tantos coches	*there is so much traffic / so many cars*
se lleva una vida tan frenética	*life is so frenetic*
la gente no se conoce	*people don't know each other*
En el campo …	*In the countryside …*
el transporte público no es fiable	*public transport is not reliable*
hay bastante desempleo	*there is quite a lot of unemployment*
no hay tantos atascos como antes	*there are not as many traffic jams as before*
yo conozco a todos mis vecinos	*I know all my neighbours*

Had a look ☐ **Nearly there** ☐ **Nailed it** ☐

¿Qué harías?	***What would you do?***
Introduciría más zonas peatonales.	*I would introduce more pedestrian areas.*
Renovaría …	*I would renovate …*
algunos edificios antiguos	*some old buildings*
las zonas deterioradas en las afueras	*the dilapidated areas on the outskirts*
Mejoraría el sistema de transporte.	*I would improve the transport system.*
Pondría / Crearía más áreas de ocio.	*I would put in / create more leisure areas.*
Construiría un nuevo centro comercial.	*I would build a new shopping centre.*
Invertiría en el turismo rural.	*I would invest in rural tourism.*
Controlaría el ruido.	*I would limit the noise.*

Had a look ☐ **Nearly there** ☐ **Nailed it** ☐

Destino Arequipa	***Destination Arequipa***
Vi / Vimos lugares interesantes.	*I saw / We saw interesting places.*
Tuvimos un guía.	*We had a guide.*
Nos hizo un recorrido.	*He/She did a tour for us.*
Nos ayudó a entender toda la historia.	*He/She helped us to understand all of the history.*
Recorrí a pie el centro histórico.	*I walked around the historic centre.*
Compré tantas cosas.	*I bought so many things.*
Alquilé una bici de montaña.	*I hired a mountain bike.*
Cogí un autobús turístico.	*I took a tourist bus.*
subimos / bajamos	*we went up / we went down*
Aprendí mucho sobre la cultura.	*I learned a lot about the culture.*
Me quedé impresionado con la ciudad.	*I was really impressed by the city.*
Había vistas maravillosas.	*There were amazing views.*
La comida estaba muy buena.	*The food was very good.*
La gente era abierta.	*The people were open.*
Lo que más me gustó fue / fueron …	*What I liked most was / were …*
¡Fue una experiencia única!	*It was a one-off experience!*
¡Qué miedo!	*What a scare!*
Volveré algún día.	*I will go back one day.*
Aprenderé a hacer surf.	*I will learn to surf.*
Trabajaré como voluntario/a.	*I will work as a volunteer.*

Had a look ☐ **Nearly there** ☐ **Nailed it** ☐

Extra words I should know for reading and listening activities

¿Qué tiempo hace?
What's the weather like?
¿Qué tiempo* hace en …? — What's the weather like in …?
está despejado — it's fine / it's cloudless
la niebla — fog
lluvioso — rainy
el pronóstico del tiempo — the weather forecast
Siempre hace buen tiempo en … — The weather is / It's always fine in …
una ola de calor — a heat wave

Had a look ☐   Nearly there ☐   Nailed it ☐

De compras
Shopping
¿Qué talla tiene? — What size are you?
¿De qué color? — What colour?
¿Cuánto es / son? — How much is it / are they?
Aquí tiene. (formal) — Here you are. (polite)
el cinturón de cuero — leather belt
el recibo — receipt
la falda — skirt
le falta un botón — a button is missing
económico/a — economical

Had a look ☐   Nearly there ☐   Nailed it ☐

¿Cómo es tu zona?
What's your area like?
árabe — Arabic
judío/a — Jewish
romano/a — Roman
el barrio — neighbourhood
la calle estrecha — narrow street
la calleja — narrow street / alley
la cordillera — mountain range
la cumbre — top (of a mountain)
el ambiente urbano — the urban environment
el espectáculo ecuestre — equestrian show
el paraíso — paradise
el teleférico — cable car
el imán — magnet

Had a look ☐   Nearly there ☐   Nailed it ☐

Verbos útiles
Useful verbs
bajar a pie — to walk down (a mountain)
caminar — to walk (in the countryside)
contemplar las vistas — to contemplate the views
esquiar — to ski / to go skiing
han mejorado / introducido / renovado / construido / creado / plantado / abierto — they have improved / introduced / renovated / built / created / planted / opened
madrugar — to get up early
merecer la pena — to be worthwhile
probarse (ropa) — to try on (clothes)
regresar — to return
tener prisa — to be in a hurry

Had a look ☐   Nearly there ☐   Nailed it ☐

Otras expresiones y palabras
Other expressions and words
a primera hora — first thing in the day
buen ojo para los negocios — a good eye for business
el empleo — employment
gratis — free (no charge)
la hora de descansar — time to have a rest
Me quedé dormido/a. — I fell asleep.
Me quedé enamorado/a de la ciudad. — I fell in love with the city.
Me quedé sin palabras. — I was speechless.
una pérdida de tiempo — a waste of time
testarudo/a como una mula** — as stubborn as a mule
el/la urbanita — city lover

Had a look ☐   Nearly there ☐   Nailed it ☐

⭐ ***Watch out for false friends**
Although *tiempo* can sometimes mean 'time', for example, *No tengo tiempo para hacer mis deberes* (I haven't got time to do my homework) in the question ¿Qué tiempo hace en …? it means 'weather'. To ask what time it is you say: ¿Qué **hora** es?

⭐ ****Try to work out the meaning of words you don't know**
Testarudo como una mula is a simile that you can translate directly into English. You only need to change one letter of *mula* to come up with 'mule' and you can then work out that *testarudo* must mean 'stubborn'.

Words I should know for speaking and writing activities

Las comidas	***Meals***
el desayuno	*breakfast*
la comida / el almuerzo	*lunch*
la merienda	*tea (meal)*
la cena	*dinner / evening meal*
desayunar	*to have breakfast / to have … for breakfast*
comer / almorzar	*to have lunch / to have … for lunch*
merendar	*to have tea / to have … for tea*
cenar	*to have dinner / to have … for dinner*
tomar	*to have (food / drink)*
beber	*to drink*
entre semana …	*during the week …*
los fines de semana …	*at weekends …*
Desayuno a las ocho.	*I have breakfast at eight o'clock.*
Desayuno / Como / Meriendo / Ceno …	*For breakfast / lunch / tea / dinner I have …*
un huevo	*an egg*

Had a look ☐ **Nearly there** ☐ **Nailed it** ☐

un yogur	*a yogurt*
un pastel	*a cake*
un bocadillo	*a sandwich*
una hamburguesa	*a hamburger*
(el) café / (el) té	*coffee / tea*
(el) Cola Cao	*Cola Cao (Spanish hot chocolate drink)*
(el) marisco	*seafood*
(el) pescado	*fish*
(el) pollo	*chicken*
(el) zumo de naranja	*orange juice*
(la) carne	*meat*
(la) ensalada	*salad*

Had a look ☐ **Nearly there** ☐ **Nailed it** ☐

(la) fruta	*fruit*
(la) leche	*milk*
(la) sopa	*soup*
(la) tortilla	*omelette*
(los) cereales	*cereals*
(los) churros	*fried doughnut sticks*
(las) galletas	*biscuits*
(las) patatas fritas	*chips*
(las) tostadas	*toast*
(las) verduras	*vegetables*
algo dulce / ligero / rápido	*something sweet / light / quick*
ser goloso/a	*to have a sweet tooth*
tener hambre	*to be hungry*
tener prisa	*to be in a hurry*
tomar un desayuno fuerte	*to have a big (lit. strong) breakfast*

Had a look ☐ **Nearly there** ☐ **Nailed it** ☐

Las expresiones de cantidad	***Expressions of quantity***
cien / quinientos gramos de …	*100 / 500 grammes of …*
un bote de …	*a jar of …*
un kilo de …	*a kilo of …*
un litro de …	*a litre of …*
un paquete de …	*a packet of …*
una barra de …	*a loaf of …*
una botella de …	*a bottle of …*
una caja de …	*a box of …*
una docena de …	*a dozen …*
una lata de …	*a tin / can of …*

Had a look ☐ **Nearly there** ☐ **Nailed it** ☐

Los alimentos	***Food products***
el aceite de oliva	*olive oil*
el agua	*water*
el ajo	*garlic*
el arroz	*rice*
el atún	*tuna*
el azúcar	*sugar*
el chorizo	*spicy sausage*
el maíz	*corn*
el pan	*bread*
el queso	*cheese*
la cerveza	*beer*
la carne de cerdo / cordero / ternera	*pork / lamb / beef*
la coliflor	*cauliflower*
la harina	*flour*
la mantequilla	*butter*
la mermelada	*jam*
los albaricoques	*apricots*
los guisantes	*peas*
los lácteos	*dairy products*
los melocotones	*peaches*

Had a look ☐ **Nearly there** ☐ **Nailed it** ☐

los melones	*melons*
los pepinos	*cucumbers*
los pimientos	*peppers*
los plátanos	*bananas*
los pomelos	*grapefruits*
los refrescos	*fizzy drinks*
las cebollas	*onions*
las fresas	*strawberries*
las judías (verdes)	*(green) beans*
las legumbres	*pulses*
las lentejas	*lentils*

las manzanas	*apples*
las naranjas	*oranges*
las peras	*pears*
las piñas	*pineapples*
las uvas	*grapes*
las zanahorias	*carrots*

Had a look ☐ **Nearly there** ☐ **Nailed it** ☐

¿Has probado ...?	*Have you tried ...?*
el gazpacho	*gazpacho (chilled soup)*
la ensaladilla rusa	*Russian salad*
la fabada	*stew of beans and pork*
Es un tipo de bebida / postre.	*It's a type of drink / dessert.*
Es un plato caliente / frío.	*It's a hot / cold dish.*
Contiene(n) ...	*It contains / They contain ...*
Fue inventado/a / introducido/a ...	*It was invented / introduced ...*

Had a look ☐ **Nearly there** ☐ **Nailed it** ☐

M 6

Mi rutina diaria — *My daily routine*

me despierto	*I wake up*
me levanto	*I get up*
me ducho	*I have a shower*
me peino	*I brush my hair*
me afeito	*I have a shave*
me visto	*I get dressed*
me lavo los dientes	*I clean my teeth*
me acuesto	*I go to bed*
salgo de casa	*I leave home*
vuelvo a casa	*I return home*
temprano / tarde	*early / late*
enseguida	*straight away*
odio levantarme	*I hate getting up*

Had a look ☐ **Nearly there** ☐ **Nailed it** ☐

¿Qué le pasa? — *What's the matter?*

No me encuentro bien.	*I don't feel well.*
Me siento fatal.	*I feel awful.*
Estoy enfermo/a / cansado/a.	*I am ill / tired.*
Tengo calor / frío.	*I am hot / cold.*
Tengo catarro.	*I have a cold.*
Tengo diarrea.	*I have diarrhoea.*
Tengo dolor de cabeza.	*I have a headache.*
Tengo fiebre.	*I have a fever / temperature.*
Tengo gripe.	*I have flu.*
Tengo mucho sueño.	*I am very sleepy.*
Tengo náuseas.	*I feel sick.*
Tengo quemaduras de sol.	*I have sunburn.*
Tengo tos.	*I have a cough.*
Tengo una insolación.	*I have sunstroke.*
Tengo una picadura.	*I've been stung.*

Had a look ☐ **Nearly there** ☐ **Nailed it** ☐

Me duele(n) ...	*My ... hurt(s).*
Me he cortado el/la ...	*I've cut my ...*
Me he hecho daño en ...	*I've hurt my ...*
Me he quemado ...	*I've burnt my ...*
Me he roto ...	*I've broken my ...*
Me he torcido ...	*I've twisted my ...*
el brazo / el estómago	*arm / stomach*
el pie / el tobillo	*foot / ankle*
la boca / la cabeza	*mouth / head*
la espalda / la garganta	*back / throat*
la mano / la nariz	*hand / nose*
la pierna / la rodilla	*leg / knee*
los dientes / las muelas	*teeth*
los oídos / las orejas	*ears*
los ojos	*eyes*

Had a look ☐ **Nearly there** ☐ **Nailed it** ☐

¿Desde hace cuánto tiempo?	*How long for?*
desde hace ...	*for ...*
un día / un mes	*a day / a month*
una hora / una semana	*an hour / a week*
¿Desde cuándo?	*Since when?*
desde ayer	*since yesterday*
desde anteayer	*since the day before yesterday*
no se preocupe	*don't worry*
¡Qué mala suerte!	*What bad luck!*
Tiene(s) que / Hay que ...	*You have to ...*
beber mucha agua	*drink lots of water*
descansar	*rest*
ir al hospital / médico / dentista	*go to the hospital / doctor / dentist*
tomar aspirinas	*take aspirins*
tomar este jarabe / estas pastillas	*take this syrup / these tablets*
usar esta crema	*use this cream*

Had a look ☐ **Nearly there** ☐ **Nailed it** ☐

Las fiestas — *Festivals*

la fiesta de ...	*the festival of ...*
esta tradición antigua ...	*this old tradition ...*
se caracteriza por ...	*is characterised by ...*
se celebra en ...	*is celebrated in ...*
se repite ...	*is repeated ...*
se queman figuras de madera	*wooden figures are burnt*
se construyen hogueras	*bonfires are built*
se disparan fuegos artificiales	*fireworks are set off*
se lanzan huevos	*eggs are thrown*
las calles se llenan de ...	*the streets are filled with ...*
los niños / los jóvenes ...	*children / young people ...*
los familiares / las familias ...	*relations / families ...*
comen manzanas de caramelo	*eat toffee apples*

decoran las casas / las tumbas con flores / velas	*decorate houses / graves with flowers / candles*
preparan linternas / altares	*prepare lanterns / altars*
se disfrazan de brujas / fantasmas	*dress up as witches / ghosts*
ven desfiles	*watch processions*

Had a look ☐ **Nearly there** ☐ **Nailed it** ☐

Un día especial	***A special day***
Abrimos los regalos.	*We open the presents.*
Buscamos huevos de chocolate.	*We look for chocolate eggs.*
Cantamos villancicos.	*We sing Christmas carols.*
Cenamos bacalao.	*We have cod for dinner.*
Comemos dulces navideños / doce uvas / pavo.	*We eat Christmas sweets / twelve grapes / turkey.*
Nos acostamos muy tarde.	*We go to bed very late.*
Nos levantamos muy temprano.	*We get up very early.*
Rezamos.	*We pray.*
Vamos a la mezquita / iglesia.	*We go to the mosque / church.*
Ayer fue …	*Yesterday was …*
el baile de fin de curso	*the school prom*
el Día de Navidad	*Christmas Day*
(el) Domingo de Pascua	*Easter Sunday*
(la) Nochebuena	*Christmas Eve*
(la) Nochevieja	*New Year's Eve*
Me bañé y luego me maquillé.	*I had a bath and then did my make-up.*

Had a look ☐ **Nearly there** ☐ **Nailed it** ☐

¿Qué va a tomar?	***What are you going to have?***
de primer / segundo plato …	*for starter / main course …*
de postre …	*for dessert …*
Voy a tomar …	*I'm going to have …*
(el) bistec	*steak*
(el) filete de cerdo	*pork fillet*
(el) flan	*crème caramel*
(el) jamón serrano	*Serrano ham*
(la) merluza en salsa verde	*hake in parsley and wine sauce*
(la) sopa de fideos	*noodle soup*
(la) tortilla de espinacas	*spinach omelette*
(la) trucha a la plancha	*grilled trout*
(los) calamares	*squid*
(las) albóndigas	*meatballs*
(las) chuletas de cordero asadas	*roast lamb chops*
(las) croquetas caseras	*home-made croquettes*
(las) gambas	*prawns*
(las) natillas	*custard*

Had a look ☐ **Nearly there** ☐ **Nailed it** ☐

¿Qué me recomienda?	*What do you recommend?*
el menú del día	*the set menu*
la especialidad de la casa	*the house speciality*
está buenísimo/a / riquísimo/a	*is extremely good / tasty*
¡Que aproveche!	*Enjoy your meal!*
¿Algo más?	*Anything else?*
Nada más, gracias.	*Nothing else, thank you.*
¿Me trae la cuenta, por favor?	*Can you bring me the bill, please?*
No tengo cuchillo / tenedor / cuchara.	*I haven't got a knife / fork / spoon.*
No hay aceite / sal / vinagre.	*There's no oil / salt / vinegar.*
El plato / vaso / mantel está sucio.	*The plate / glass / table cloth is dirty.*
El vino está malo.	*The wine is bad / off.*
La carne está fría.	*The meat is cold.*
dejar una propina	*to leave a tip*
equivocarse	*to make a mistake*
pedir	*to order / to ask for*
ser alérgico/a …	*to be allergic to …*
ser vegetariano/a	*to be a vegetarian*

Had a look ☐ **Nearly there** ☐ **Nailed it** ☐

Un festival de música	***A music festival***
Me fascina(n) …	*…fascinate(s) me.*
Admiro …	*I admire …*
No aguanto / soporto …	*I can't stand …*
su actitud / talento	*his/her attitude / talent*
su comportamiento	*his/her behaviour*
su determinación / estilo	*his/her determination / style*
su forma de vestir	*his/her way of dressing*
su música / voz	*his/her music / voice*
sus canciones / coreografías	*his/her songs / choreography*
sus ideas / letras	*his/her ideas / lyrics*
atrevido/a(s)	*daring*
imaginativo/a(s)	*imaginative*
precioso/a(s)	*beautiful*
repetitivo/a(s)	*repetitive*
original(es)	*original*
triste(s)	*sad*
Me/Te hace(n) falta …	*I/You need …*
crema solar	*sun cream*
el pasaporte / DNI	*your passport / national ID card*
un sombrero / una gorra	*a hat / cap*

Had a look ☐ **Nearly there** ☐ **Nailed it** ☐

Extra words I should know for reading and listening activities

Verbos y expresiones útiles	*Useful verbs and expressions*
prestar atención	*to pay attention*
romperse (el brazo)*	*to break (your arm)*
torcerse (el tobillo)*	*to twist (your ankle)*
sentirse mal	*to feel bad / to not feel very well*
hacerse daño	*to hurt yourself*
doblar servilletas	*to fold serviettes*
atraer	*to attract*
sufrir acidentes domésticos	*to have domestic accidents*
concienciar	*to raise awareness*
aprobar	*to approve*
montar una tienda	*to put up a tent*
sin contar	*not counting*
Estas gambas están buenísimas.**	*These prawns are extremely good.*
No me quedé nada decepcionado/a.	*I wasn't at all disappointed.*

Had a look ☐ Nearly there ☐ Nailed it ☐

Alimentos y comidas	*Food products and meals*
Apto para alérgicos / celiacos e intolerancias alimentarias.	*Suitable for people with allergies / reactions / celiacs and food intolerances.*
el asado de pavo	*roast turkey dinner*
el bufé libre	*self-service buffet*
la comida rápida / sencilla de preparar	*fast / convenience food*
las delicias culinarias	*culinary treats*
la dieta mediterránea / equilibrada / sana	*Mediterranean / balanced / healthy diet*
el guiso	*stew*
el horno	*oven*
la intoxicación alimentaria	*food poisoning*
los mazapanes	*marzipan sweets*

Had a look ☐ Nearly there ☐ Nailed it ☐

***Use the definite article to say you have hurt / broken / twisted / cut or burned something**

In Spanish the definite article *el* or *la* is used with verbs such as *romperse* (to break), *torcerse* (to twist), *doler* (to hurt), *cortarse* (to cut oneself) and *quemarse* (to burn oneself), for example:
Me he roto **la** *pierna.* → I've broken **my** leg.
Se ha torcido **el** *tobillo.* → He/She has twisted **her** ankle.
Me duele **la** *cabeza.* → **My** head aches.
Note too that *doler* is a stem-changing word and *romperse* an irregular verb — the past participle is *roto.*

Fiestas y celebraciones	*Festivals and celebrations*
acceso para minusválidos	*wheelchair access*
el belén	*nativity scene*
las bodas de plata	*silver wedding*
la calavera	*skull*
la campanada	*stroke of the bell*
el DNI (Documento Nacional de Identidad)	*identity card*
la edad mínima	*minimum age*
el encierro	*bull running*
el fracaso de la conspiración de la pólvora	*gunpower plot*
las luces navideñas	*Christmas lights*
la medianoche	*midnight*
la muñeca	*doll*
el peligro	*danger*
los poseedores de abono de 2 / 3 o 4 días	*those who have a ticket for 2 / 3 or 4 days*
la pulsera	*bracelet*
la quinceañera	*15-year-old girl (in Latin American countries they have a big celebration when a girl turns 15)*
los seres queridos	*loved ones*
el sinfín	*endless number*
el tintineo	*ringing (of mobile phone)*
truco o trato	*trick or treat*
la población indígena	*the indigenous population*

Had a look ☐ Nearly there ☐ Nailed it ☐

Adjetivos útiles	*Useful adjectives*
sabroso/a	*tasty*
picante / salado/a	*spicy / salty*
asqueroso/a	*disgusting*
orgulloso/a	*proud*
torpe	*clumsy*
encantador(a)	*charming*
al ajillo	*cooked with garlic*
andino/a	*Andean*
caribeño/a	*Caribbean*
ubicado/a	*situated*
compuesto/a de …	*which has … in it*

Had a look ☐ Nearly there ☐ Nailed it ☐

****How to make adjectives stronger**

To say really (nice), extremely (expensive), etc. add *-ísimo* to the end of the adjective, and make it agree, for example, *Este ejercicio es facil**ísimo*** (This exercise is really easy). If the adjective ends in a vowel, remove the vowel before adding the ending, so, for example, *bueno* becomes *buen**ísimo*** and *importante* becomes *important**ísimo***.

Words I should know for speaking and writing activities

¿En qué trabajas?	***What is your job?***
Soy … / Es …	*I am … / He/She is …*
Me gustaría ser …	*I would like to be a…*
abogado/a	*lawyer*
albañil	*bricklayer / builder*
amo/a de casa	*househusband / housewife*
azafato/a	*flight attendant*
bailarín / bailarina	*dancer*
bombero/a	*firefighter*
camarero/a	*waiter / waitress*
cantante	*singer*
cocinero/a	*cook*
contable	*accountant*
dependiente/a	*shop assistant*
diseñador(a)	*designer*

Had a look ☐ **Nearly there** ☐ **Nailed it** ☐

electricista	*electrician*
enfermero/a	*nurse*
escritor(a)	*writer*
fontanero/a	*plumber*
fotógrafo/a	*photographer*
funcionario/a	*civil servant*
guía turístico/a	*tour guide*
ingeniero/a	*engineer*
jardinero/a	*gardener*
mecánico/a	*mechanic*
médico/a	*doctor*
músico/a	*musician*
peluquero/a	*hairdresser*
periodista	*journalist*
policía	*police officer*
profesor(a)	*teacher*
recepcionista	*receptionist*
socorrista	*lifeguard*
soldado	*soldier*
veterinario/a	*vet*

Had a look ☐ **Nearly there** ☐ **Nailed it** ☐

Es un trabajo …	*It's a … job*
artístico / emocionante	*artistic / exciting*
exigente / importante	*demanding / important*
fácil / difícil	*easy / difficult*
manual / monótono	*manual / monotonous*
variado / repetitivo	*varied / repetitive*
con responsabilidad	*with responsibility*
con buenas perspectivas	*with good prospects*
con un buen sueldo	*with a good salary*

Had a look ☐ **Nearly there** ☐ **Nailed it** ☐

Tengo que … / Suelo …	*I have to … / I tend to …*
cuidar a los clientes / pacientes / pasajeros	*look after the customers / patients / passengers*
contestar llamadas telefónicas	*answer telephone calls*
cuidar las plantas y las flores	*look after the plants and flowers*
enseñar / vigilar a los niños	*teach / supervise the children*
hacer entrevistas	*do interviews*
preparar platos distintos	*prepare different dishes*
reparar coches	*repair cars*
servir comida y bebida	*serve food and drink*
trabajar en un taller / en un hospital / en una tienda / a bordo de un avión	*work in a workshop / in a hospital / in a shop / aboard a plane*
vender ropa de marca	*sell designer clothing*
viajar por todo el mundo	*travel the world*

Had a look ☐ **Nearly there** ☐ **Nailed it** ☐

¿Qué tipo de persona eres?	***What type of person are you?***
Creo que soy …	*I think I'm …*
ambicioso/a	*ambitious*
comprensivo/a	*understanding*
creativo/a	*creative*
extrovertido/a	*extroverted / outgoing*
fuerte	*strong*
inteligente	*intelligent*
organizado/a	*organised*
paciente	*patient*
práctico/a	*practical*
serio/a	*serious*
trabajador(a)	*hardworking*
valiente	*brave*

Had a look ☐ **Nearly there** ☐ **Nailed it** ☐

¿Qué haces para ganar dinero?	***What do you do to earn money?***
¿Tienes un trabajo a tiempo parcial?	*Do you have a part-time job?*
Reparto periódicos.	*I deliver newspapers.*
Hago de canguro.	*I babysit.*
Trabajo de cajero/a.	*I work as a cashier.*
Ayudo con las tareas domésticas.	*I help with the housework.*
Cocino.	*I cook.*
Lavo los platos.	*I wash the dishes.*
Paso la aspiradora.	*I do the vacuuming.*
Plancho la ropa.	*I iron the clothes.*
Pongo y quito la mesa.	*I lay and clear the table.*
Paseo al perro.	*I walk the dog.*
Corto el césped.	*I cut the lawn.*

Had a look ☐ **Nearly there** ☐ **Nailed it** ☐

Lo hago …	*I do it …*
los sábados	*on Saturdays*
antes / después del insti	*before / after school*
cuando necesito dinero	*when I need money*

M 7

cuando mi madre está trabajando	*when my mum is working*
cuando me necesitan	*when they need me*
cada mañana	*each / every morning*
una vez / dos veces a la semana	*once / twice a week*
Gano … euros / libras a la hora / al día / a la semana.	*I earn … euros / pounds per hour / day / week.*
Me llevo bien con mis compañeros.	*I get on well with my colleagues.*
Mi jefe/a es amable.	*My boss is nice.*
El horario es flexible.	*The hours are flexible.*

Had a look ☐ **Nearly there** ☐ **Nailed it** ☐

Mis prácticas laborales — *Work experience*

Hice mis prácticas laborales en …	*I did my work experience in …*
Pasé quince días trabajando en …	*I spent a fortnight working in …*
un polideportivo	*a sports centre*
una agencia de viajes / una granja	*a travel agency / a farm*
una escuela / una oficina	*a school / an office*
una fábrica de juguetes	*a toy factory*
una tienda benéfica / solidaria	*a charity shop*
la empresa de mi madre	*my mum's company*

Had a look ☐ **Nearly there** ☐ **Nailed it** ☐

El primer / último día conocí a / llegué …	*On the first / last day I met / I arrived …*
Cada día / Todos los días …	*Each / Every day …*
archivaba documentos	*I filed documents*
ayudaba …	*I helped …*
cogía el autobús / el metro	*I caught the bus / underground*
empezaba / terminaba a las …	*I started / finished at …*
hacía una variedad de tareas	*I did a variety of tasks*
iba en transporte público	*I went by public transport*
llevaba ropa elegante	*I wore smart clothes*
ponía folletos en los estantes	*I put brochures on the shelves*
sacaba fotocopias	*I did photocopying*

Had a look ☐ **Nearly there** ☐ **Nailed it** ☐

Mi jefe/a era …	*My boss was …*
Mis compañeros eran …	*My colleagues were …*
Los clientes eran …	*The customers were …*
alegre(s)	*cheerful*
(des)agradable(s)	*(un)pleasant*
(mal)educado/a(s)	*polite (rude)*
El trabajo era duro.	*The job was hard.*

Aprendí …	*I learned …*
muchas nuevas habilidades	*lots of new skills*
a trabajar en equipo	*to work in a team*
a usar …	*to use …*
No aprendí nada nuevo.	*I didn't learn anything new.*

Had a look ☐ **Nearly there** ☐ **Nailed it** ☐

¿Por qué aprender idiomas? — *Why learn languages?*

Aumenta tu confianza.	*It increases your confidence.*
Estimula el cerebro.	*It stimulates the brain.*
Mejora tus perspectivas laborales.	*It improves your job prospects.*
Te abre la mente.	*It opens your mind.*
Te hace parecer más atractivo.	*It makes you appear more attractive.*
Te ayuda a …	*It helps you to …*
Te permite …	*It allows you to …*
apreciar la vida cultural de otros países	*appreciate the cultural life of other countries*
conocer a mucha gente distinta	*meet lots of different people*
conocer nuevos sitios	*get to know new places*
encontrar un trabajo	*find a job*
descubrir nuevas culturas	*discover new cultures*
establecer buenas relaciones	*establish good relationships*
hacer nuevos amigos	*make new friends*
mejorar tu lengua materna	*improve your first language*
solucionar problemas	*solve problems*
trabajar o estudiar en el extranjero	*work or study abroad*
Me hace falta saber hablar idiomas extranjeros.	*I need to know how to speak foreign languages.*
(No) Domino el inglés.	*I (don't) speak English fluently.*
Hablo un poco de ruso.	*I speak a bit of Russian.*

Had a look ☐ **Nearly there** ☐ **Nailed it** ☐

Solicitando un trabajo — *Applying for a job*

Se busca / Se requiere …	*… required.*
(No) Hace falta experiencia.	*Experience (not) needed.*
Muy señor mío	*Dear Sir*
Le escribo para solicitar el puesto de …	*I'm writing to apply for the post of …*
Le adjunto mi currículum vitae.	*I'm enclosing my CV.*
Le agradezco su amable atención.	*Thank you for your kind attention.*
Atentamente	*Yours sincerely / faithfully*

M 7

Me apetece trabajar en …	*Working in … appeals to me.*
(No) Tengo experiencia previa.	*I (don't) have previous experience.*
He estudiado / trabajado …	*I've studied / worked …*
He hecho un curso de …	*I've done a course in …*
Tengo …	*I have …*
buen sentido del humor	*a good sense of humour*
buenas capacidades de comunicación / resolución de problemas	*good communication / problem-solving skills*
buenas habilidades lingüísticas	*good language skills*

Had a look ☐ **Nearly there** ☐ **Nailed it** ☐

Un año sabático	***A gap year***
Si pudiera tomarme un año sabático …	*If I could take a gap year …*
Si tuviera bastante dinero …	*If I had enough money …*
apoyaría un proyecto medioambiental	*I would support an environmental project*
aprendería a esquiar	*I would learn to ski*
ayudaría a construir un colegio	*I would help to build a school*
buscaría un trabajo	*I would look for a job*
enseñaría inglés	*I would teach English*
ganaría mucho dinero	*I would earn a lot of money*
haría un viaje en Interrail	*I would go Interrailing*
iría a España / donde …	*I would go to Spain / where …*
mejoraría mi nivel de español	*I would improve my level of Spanish*
nunca olvidaría la experiencia	*I would never forget the experience*
pasaría un año en …	*I would spend a year in …*
trabajaría en un orfanato	*I would work in an orphanage*
viajaría con mochila por el mundo	*I would go backpacking around the world*

Had a look ☐ **Nearly there** ☐ **Nailed it** ☐

¿Cómo viajarías?	***How would you travel?***
Cogería el / Viajaría en autobús / autocar / avión / tren.	*I would catch the / travel by bus / coach / plane / train.*
Es más barato / cómodo / rápido.	*It's cheaper / more comfortable / quicker.*
Puedes …	*You can …*
ver vídeos mientras viajas	*watch videos whilst you travel*
dejar tu maleta en la consigna	*leave your suitcase in the left-luggage office*
Hay muchos / pocos atascos / retrasos …	*There are lots of / few traffic jams / delays …*
en las autopistas / las carreteras	*on the motorways / roads*
Los billetes son carísimos.	*The tickets are extremely expensive.*
Los conductores están en huelga.	*The drivers are on strike.*
Odio esperar en la parada de autobús.	*I hate waiting at the bus stop.*
Tengo miedo a volar.	*I'm scared of flying.*

Had a look ☐ **Nearly there** ☐ **Nailed it** ☐

Viajando en tren	***Travelling by train***
El tren con destino a … efectuará su salida … de la vía / del andén dos	*The train to … will leave / depart … from platform two*
el (tren) AVE	*high-speed train*
la taquilla	*the ticket office*
Quisiera un billete de ida a …	*I would like a single ticket to …*
Quisiera un billete de ida y vuelta a …	*I would like a return ticket to …*
¿De qué andén sale?	*From which platform does it leave?*
¿A qué hora sale / llega?	*What time does it leave / arrive?*
¿Es directo o hay que cambiar?	*Is it direct or do I have to change?*

Had a look ☐ **Nearly there** ☐ **Nailed it** ☐

El futuro	***The future***
Me interesa(n) …	*…interest(s) me.*
Me importa(n) …	*…matter(s) to me.*
Me preocupa(n) …	*…worry / worries me.*
el desempleo / el paro	*unemployment*
el dinero / el éxito	*money / success*
el fracaso / el matrimonio	*failure / marriage*
la responsabilidad	*responsibility*
la independencia / la pobreza	*independence / poverty*
los niños / las notas	*children / marks*
Espero …	*I hope to …*
Me gustaría …	*I would like to …*
Pienso …	*I plan to / intend to …*
Quiero …	*I want to …*
Tengo la intención de …	*I intend to …*
Voy a …	*I am going to …*

Had a look ☐ **Nearly there** ☐ **Nailed it** ☐

aprender a conducir	*learn to drive*
aprobar mis exámenes	*pass my exams*
casarme	*get married*
conseguir un buen empleo / trabajo	*get a good job*
estudiar una carrera universitaria	*study a university course*
montar mi propio negocio	*set up my own business*

M 7

sacar buenas notas	*get good marks*
ser feliz	*be happy*
tener hijos	*have children*
trabajar como voluntario/a	*work as a volunteer*
Cuando …	*When …*
gane bastante dinero …	*I earn enough money …*
me enamore …	*I fall in love …*
sea mayor …	*I'm older …*
tenga … años …	*I'm … years old …*
vaya a la universidad …	*I go to university …*
termine este curso / el bachillerato / la formación profesional / la licenciatura …	*I finish this course / my A Levels / my vocational course / my degree …*
buscaré un trabajo	*I will look for a job*
compartiré piso con …	*I will share a flat with …*
compraré un coche / una casa	*I will buy a car / house*
iré a otro insti / a la universidad	*I will go to another school / to university*
me casaré	*I will get married*
me iré de casa	*I will leave home*
seguiré estudiando en mi insti	*I will carry on studying at my school*
seré famoso/a	*I will be famous*
me tomaré un año sabático	*I will take a gap year*
trabajaré como …	*I will work as …*

Had a look ☐ **Nearly there** ☐ **Nailed it** ☐

Extra words I should know for reading and listening activities

Verbos útiles	***Useful verbs***
ahorrar	*to save (up)*
alistarse en el ejército	*to enlist in the army*
aprovechar	*to make the most of*
arreglar (una habitación)	*to tidy (a room)*
barrer las hojas	*to sweep up leaves*
buscar un trabajo como …	*to look for a job as a …*
cortar el pelo	*to cut hair*
cumplir un sueño	*to make a dream come true*
descuidar	*to neglect*
obtener el título de	*to qualify as …*
estar harto/a de	*to be fed up with*
mantener el equilibrio	*to maintain the balance*
merecer / valer la pena	*to be worthwhile*
ordeñar (una vaca)	*to milk (a cow)*
quitar la nieve	*to clear the snow*
trabajar al aire libre	*to work outside*
viajar como mochilero/a*	*to go backpacking*

Had a look ☐ **Nearly there** ☐ **Nailed it** ☐

El mundo laboral	***The world of work***
el/la amo/a de casa	*househusband / housewife*
el/la animador(a)	*events organiser / entertainer*
el anuncio	*advertisement*
la antigüedad	*number of years spent in a job*
el/la corresponsal de guerra	*war correspondent*
el curso de formación	*training course*
el curso de primeros auxilios	*first aid course*
el curso optativo (de pastelería, etc.)	*optional (pastry-making, etc.) course*
el departamento de ventas	*sales department*
el descanso	*break*
la deuda	*debt*
la emisora de radio	*radio station*
el/la empleado/a	*employee*
la fiesta de despedida	*farewell party*
la gestión administrativa	*business management*
la hostelería	*hotel industry*
el/la ingeniero/a de sonido	*sound engineer*
la manera de vestir	*the way you dress*
el medio ambiente	*the environment*
el oficio	*trade / profession*
el paquete de beneficios	*benefits package*
las perspectivas	*prospects*
el plan de seguro médico	*medical insurance*
la reunión	*meeting*
un salario bajo / alto / justo	*a low / high / fair wage / salary*
la sanidad	*health*
la seguridad	*safety*
el trabajo de mis sueños	*my dream job*
el voluntariado	*volunteering*

Had a look ☐ **Nearly there** ☐ **Nailed it** ☐

Had a look ☐ **Nearly there** ☐ **Nailed it** ☐

Otras frases y palabras útiles	***Other useful phrases and words***
cariñoso/a	*affectionate*
cuando cumplas cinco años en la empresa	*when you have worked for five years in the company*
en referencia a	*with reference to*
experiencia deseable	*experience desirable*
honrado/a	*honest*
Me da la oportunidad de …	*It gives me the chance to …*
Me trataban como un esclavo.	*They treated me like a slave.*
No soporto a mi jefe.	*I can't stand my boss.*
¡Ojalá no fuera tan peligroso!	*I wish it wasn't so dangerous.*
salario a convenir	*salary to be agreed*
Serías un buen … / una buena …	*You would be a good …*
subvencionado/a	*subsidised*
¿Te apetece …?**	*Do you fancy …?*

Had a look ☐ **Nearly there** ☐ **Nailed it** ☐

M 7

***Work out meanings of unfamiliar words**
When trying to work out the meaning of a new word look for clues – think Context, Cognates, Common sense. For example, if you know the word *mochila* (backpack), you should be able to work out that *viajar como mochilero* would literally translate 'to travel as a backpacker'.

****Memorise and adapt useful phrases**
Learn useful phrases and adapt them to different contexts. You can use *¿Te apetece …?* to ask a friend what he or she would like to do.
Example: *¿Te apetece ir al cine?* (Do you fancy going to the cinema?)
And you could adapt it to say what you would fancy doing.
Example: *Me apetece salir esta noche.* (I fancy going out tonight).

Words I should know for speaking and writing activities

¿Cómo es tu casa?	*What is your house like?*
Vivo en …	*I live in …*
un bloque de pisos	*a block of flats*
una casa individual	*a detached house*
una casa adosada	*a semi-detached / terraced house*
una residencia de ancianos	*an old people's home*
una finca / granja	*a farmhouse*
Alquilamos una casa amueblada.	*We rent a furnished house.*
Está en …	*It is in / on …*
un barrio de la ciudad	*a district / suburb of the city / town*
las afueras	*the outskirts*
el campo	*the country*
la costa	*the coast*
la montaña / sierra	*the mountains*
el cuarto piso de un edificio antiguo	*the fourth floor of an old building*

Had a look ☐ **Nearly there** ☐ **Nailed it** ☐

Mi apartamento / piso tiene …	*My apartment / flat has …*
tres dormitorios	*three bedrooms*
dos cuartos de baño	*two bathrooms*
una cocina amplia y bien equipada	*a spacious / well-equipped kitchen*
un comedor recién renovado	*a recently refurbished dining room*
un estudio	*a study*
un aseo	*a toilet*
un sótano	*a basement / cellar*
un salón	*a living room*
una mesa	*a table*
unas sillas	*some chairs*
Mi casa ideal sería …	*My ideal house would be …*
Tendría …	*It would have …*
una piscina climatizada	*a heated swimming pool*
mi propio cine en casa	*my own home cinema*
una sala de fiestas	*a party room*
Cambiaría los muebles.	*I would change the furniture.*
Pintaría … de otro color.	*I would paint … another colour.*

Had a look ☐ **Nearly there** ☐ **Nailed it** ☐

¿Cómo se debería cuidar el medio ambiente en casa?	*How should you look after the environment at home?*
Para cuidar el medio ambiente se debería …	*To care for the environment you / one should …*
apagar la luz	*turn off the light*
ducharse en vez de bañarse	*have a shower instead of taking a bath*
separar la basura	*separate the rubbish*
reciclar el plástico y el vidrio	*recycle plastic and glass*
desenchufar los aparatos eléctricos	*unplug electric appliances*
ahorrar energía	*save energy*
cerrar el grifo	*turn off the tap*
hacer todo lo posible	*do everything possible*
no se debería …	*you / one should not …*
malgastar el agua	*waste water*
usar bolsas de plástico	*use plastic bags*

Had a look ☐ **Nearly there** ☐ **Nailed it** ☐

¿Cuáles son los problemas globales más serios hoy en día?	*What are the most serious global issues today?*
Me preocupa(n) …	*I am worried about …*
el paro / desempleo	*unemployment*
el hambre / la pobreza	*hunger / poverty*
la deforestación	*deforestation*
la diferencia entre ricos y pobres	*the difference between rich and poor*
la drogadicción / la salud / la obesidad	*drug addiction / health / obesity*
la crisis económica	*the economic crisis*
los problemas del medio ambiente	*environmental problems*
los sin hogar / techo	*the homeless*
los animales en peligro de extinción	*animals in danger of extinction*

Had a look ☐ **Nearly there** ☐ **Nailed it** ☐

Es necesario / esencial que …	*It's necessary / essential that (we) …*
cuidemos el planeta	*look after the planet*
hagamos proyectos de conservación	*do conservation projects*
compremos / usemos productos verdes / de comercio justo	*buy / use green / fairtrade products*
apoyemos proyectos de ayuda	*support aid projects*
creemos oportunidades de trabajo	*create job opportunities*
ayudemos a evitar el consumo de sustancias perjudiciales	*help to avoid the consumption of harmful substances*
ahorremos agua	*save water*
construyamos más casas	*build more houses*
cambiemos la ley	*change the law*
consumamos menos	*consume less*
hagamos campañas publicitarias	*carry out publicity campaigns*

recaudemos dinero para organizaciones de caridad en el tercer mundo	*raise money for charities in the third world*
No es justo / Es terrible que haya …	*It's not fair / It's terrible that there is …*
tanta desigualdad social / contaminación	*so much social inequality / pollution*
tanta gente sin trabajo y sin techo	*so many people out of work and homeless*
tanta gente obesa y tantos drogadictos	*so many obese people and so many drug addicts*

Had a look ☐ **Nearly there** ☐ **Nailed it** ☐

¡Actúa localmente!	***Act locally!***
Hay demasiada …	*There is / are too much / many …*
basura en las calles	*rubbish on the streets*
gente sin espacio para vivir	*people with nowhere to live*
destrucción de los bosques	*destruction of woodland / forest*
polución de los mares y ríos	*pollution of seas and rivers*
El aire está contaminado.	*The air is polluted.*
Los combustibles fósiles se acaban.	*Fossil fuels are running out.*
No corte tantos árboles.	*Don't cut down so many trees.*
No vaya en coche si es posible ir a pie.	*Don't go by car if it's possible to walk.*
No tire basura al suelo.	*Don't throw rubbish onto the ground.*
No malgaste energía.	*Don't waste energy.*
No construya tantas casas grandes.	*Don't build so many large houses.*
No eche tantos desechos químicos.	*Don't release so much chemical waste.*
Plante más bosques y selvas.	*Plant more woods and forests.*
Reduzca las emisiones de los vehículos.	*Reduce vehicle emissions.*
Recicle el papel, el vidrio y el plástico.	*Recycle paper, glass and plastic.*
Use energías renovables.	*Use renewable energies.*
Diseñe casas más pequeñas.	*Design smaller houses.*
Introduzca leyes más estrictas.	*Introduce stricter laws.*

Had a look ☐ **Nearly there** ☐ **Nailed it** ☐

llevar una vida más verde	*(to) live a greener life*
salvar el planeta	*(to) save the planet*
reducir la huella de carbono	*(to) reduce your carbon footprint*
ecológico/a	*environmentally-friendly*
el techo	*roof*
el agua de lluvia	*rain water*
el domicilio	*home*
los recursos naturales	*natural resources*
los paneles solares	*solar panels*
la arena	*sand*
los (eco-)ladrillos	*(eco-)bricks*
una fábrica	*a factory*
mudarse (de casa)	*(to) move house*

Had a look ☐ **Nearly there** ☐ **Nailed it** ☐

Una dieta sana	***A healthy diet***
los alimentos	*foods*
lácteos	*milk products*
carne / pescados y huevos	*meat / fish and eggs*
frutas y verduras	*fruit and vegetables*
cereales	*cereals*
fideos	*noodles*
grasas	*fats*
dulces	*sugars / sweet things*
legumbres	*pulses*
frutos secos	*nuts and dried fruit*
los nutrientes	*nutrients*
proteínas	*proteins*
minerales	*minerals*
grasa	*fat*
sal	*salt*
vitaminas	*vitamins*
azúcar	*sugar*
gluten	*gluten*
el sabor	*taste*

Had a look ☐ **Nearly there** ☐ **Nailed it** ☐

vegetariano / vegano	*vegetarian / vegan*
saludable / sano / malsano	*healthy / healthy / unhealthy*
(No) Tengo hambre / sed / sueño.	*I am (not) hungry / thirsty / tired.*
tiempo para cocinar	*time to cook*
contiene / contienen	*it contains / they contain*
La fibra …	*Fibre …*
protege contra el cáncer	*protects against cancer*
combate la obesidad	*combats obesity*
reduce el riesgo de enfermedades	*reduces the risk of diseases*
evitar comer / beber	*avoid eating / drinking*
cambiar mi dieta	*change my diet*
llevar una dieta equilibrada	*have a balanced diet*
preparar con ingredientes frescos	*prepare with fresh ingredients*
engordar	*to put on weight*
saltarse el desayuno	*to skip breakfast*
practicar más deporte	*to do more sport*

Had a look ☐ **Nearly there** ☐ **Nailed it** ☐

¡Vivir a tope!	***Live life to the full***
Beber alcohol …	*Drinking alcohol …*
Fumar cigarrillos / porros …	*To smoke / Smoking cigarettes / joints …*
Tomar drogas blandas / duras …	*To take / Taking soft / hard drugs …*
Es / No es …	*It is / isn't …*
ilegal / peligroso	*illegal / dangerous*
un malgasto de dinero	*a waste of money*
una tontería / un problema serio	*stupid / a serious problem*
un vicio muy caro	*an expensive habit*
muy perjudicial para la salud	*very damaging to your health*
tan malo	*as bad*
provoca mal aliento	*causes bad breath*
daña los pulmones	*damages the lungs*
mancha los dientes de amarillo	*stains your teeth yellow*
causa el fracaso escolar / depresión	*causes failure at school / depression*
produce una fuerte dependencia física	*produces a strong, physical dependence*
tiene muchos riesgos	*has many risks*
afecta a tu capacidad para tomar decisiones	*affects your capacity to make decisions*
te relaja / te quita el estrés	*relaxes you / relieves stress*
te quita el sueño / control	*robs you of sleep / self-control*
te hace sentir bien / más adulto	*makes you feel good / more adult*

Had a look ☐ **Nearly there** ☐ **Nailed it** ☐

Es fácil engancharse.	*It's easy to get hooked.*
¡Qué asco!	*How disgusting!*
Cedí ante la presión de grupo.	*I gave in to peer pressure.*
Caí en el hábito de …	*I fell into the habit of …*
Empecé a …	*I started to …*
Perdí peso.	*I lost weight.*
No puedo parar.	*I can't stop.*
Ya he empezado a …	*I've already started to …*
Todavía no he dejado de …	*I still haven't given up …*
A partir de ahora intentaré …	*From now on I will try to …*

Had a look ☐ **Nearly there** ☐ **Nailed it** ☐

¡El deporte nos une!	***Sport unites us!***
¿Para qué sirven …?	*What are … for?*
los eventos deportivos internacionales	*international sporting events*
los grandes acontecimientos deportivos	*big sporting events*
los Juegos Paralímpicos / Olímpicos	*the Paralympics / Olympics*
la Copa Mundial del Fútbol	*the Football World Cup*
Sirven para …	*They serve to …*
promover …	*promote / foster / encourage …*
la participación en el deporte	*participation in sport*
el espíritu de solidaridad	*team spirit*
regenerar los centros urbanos	*regenerate city centres*
elevar el orgullo nacional	*increase national pride*
transmitir los valores de respeto y disciplina	*convey / instil the values of respect and discipline*
unir a la gente	*unite people*
dar un impulso económico	*give a boost to the economy*
inspirar a la gente	*inspire people*

Had a look ☐ **Nearly there** ☐ **Nailed it** ☐

Una / Otra desventaja es …	*A / Another disadvantage is …*
el riesgo de ataques terroristas	*the risk of terrorist attacks*
el tráfico	*the traffic*
el dopaje	*doping*
la deuda	*the debt*
el coste de organización de la seguridad	*the cost of organising the security*
la ciudad anfitriona	*the host city*
el voluntariado	*volunteering*
Solicité un trabajo voluntario porque …	*I applied for a volunteering job because …*
(Nunca) Había sido …	*I had (never) been …*
Antes ya había trabajado como …	*Previously I had already worked as …*

Had a look ☐ **Nearly there** ☐ **Nailed it** ☐

¡Apúntate!	***Sign up!***
¿Qué estabas haciendo?	*What were you doing?*
Estaba / Estábamos / Estaban …	*I/He/She/It was / We were / They were …*
ensayando	*rehearsing*
nevando	*snowing*
entrando en casa	*coming into the house*
durmiendo	*sleeping*
conduciendo por la ciudad	*driving through the city*
leyendo	*reading*
volando por el aire	*flying through the air*
Se estaba convirtiendo en un río.	*It was turning into a river.*
Se estaba moviendo.	*It was moving.*
a mi alrededor	*around me*
Se estaban cayendo.	*They were falling.*
¿Cómo te enteraste del/ de la/de las …?	*How did you find out about the …?*
temblor	*tremor*

incendio forestal	*forest fire*
huracán	*hurricane*
tornado	*tornado*
terremoto	*earthquake*
tormenta de nieve	*snow storm*
acción humanitaria	*humanitarian campaign*
inundaciones	*floods*

Had a look ☐ **Nearly there** ☐ **Nailed it** ☐

Estaba …	*He/She was …*
mirando / viendo las noticias / la tele	*watching the news / the TV*
buscando informaciones en línea	*looking for information online*
charlando con un amigo / una amiga	*chatting with a friend*
leyendo un post en Facebook	*reading a Facebook post*
cuando …	*when …*
encontré un reportaje / un artículo	*I found a report / an article*
recibí un SMS	*I received a text message*
(lo) vi en las noticias	*I saw (it) on the news*
mi novio me llamó / me contó la historia	*my boyfriend called me / told me the story*

Had a look ☐ **Nearly there** ☐ **Nailed it** ☐

una organización de servicio voluntario	*a voluntary organisation*
una campaña para las víctimas	*a campaign for the victims*
una caja de supervivencia	*a survival box*
Decidí apuntarme.	*I decided to sign up.*
recaudar fondos / solicitar donativos	*to raise funds / to ask for donations*
organizamos algunos eventos	*we organised some events*
un concierto / un espectáculo de baile	*a concert / a dance show*
una carrera de bici apadrinada	*a sponsored bike race*
una venta de pasteles	*a cake sale*
ser solidario	*showing solidarity / supporting*
Te hace sentir más conectado con los demás.	*It makes you feed more connected to others.*

Had a look ☐ **Nearly there** ☐ **Nailed it** ☐

M 8

Extra words I should know for reading and listening activities

Verbos útiles	***Useful verbs***
afiliarse a un club	*to join a club*
aprovechar una experiencia previa	*to make the most of a previous experience*
asomarse por la ventana	*to look out of a window*
colaborar en un evento	*to take part in an event*
conseguir hacer algo	*to manage to do something*
crear conciencia	*to raise consciousness*
darse cuenta	*to realise*
dedicar tiempo	*to spend time*
dejar de fumar / beber / tomar drogas	*to give up smoking / drinking / taking drugs*
demostrar	*to demonstrate*
desarrollar	*to develop*
destruir (la selva)	*to destroy (the rainforest)*
emborracharse	*to get drunk*

Had a look ☐ **Nearly there** ☐ **Nailed it** ☐

fomentar el espíritu de solidaridad	*to promote a spirit of solidarity*
frenar	*to stop / to break*
hacer una revisión de algo	*to check something (over)*
instalarse	*to settle*
ir de carreras	*to race*
llevarse (algo) a la tumba	*to take (something) to the grave*
mantenerse en forma	*to keep fit*
Me queda mucho por hacer.	*I've got a long way to go. / I've still got a lot to do.*
ocuparse de	*to be in charge of*
provocar molestias	*to cause annoyance*
quitar la vida a alguien	*to cause someone to die*
recoger	*to collect*
tener para comer	*to have enough to eat*

Had a look ☐ **Nearly there** ☐ **Nailed it** ☐

***How to spot opposites**

In English 'un-' is often used before an adjective to give the opposite, for example: forgettable → **un**forgettable. In Spanish *in-* is used in the same way, for example: *olvidable* (you may already know that *olvidar* means 'to forget') → ***in**olvidable*. Some other examples are:

capaz → ***in**capaz*
eficiente → ***in**eficiente*
feliz → ***in**feliz*
justo → ***in**justo*

See if you can think of some more. You could use a dictionary to help you.

Nombres útiles	***Useful nouns***
el agua potable	*drinking water*
el banco de alimentos	*food bank*
la caminata patrocinada	*sponsored walk*
el/la compatriota	*fellow countryman / countrywoman*
la confianza en sí mismo/a	*self-confidence*
el entorno	*surrounding area*
la escasez	*shortage / scarcity*
una experiencia inolvidable*	*an unforgettable experience*
la falta (de algo)	*the lack (of something)*
los hidratos de carbono	*carbohydrates*
jóvenes y jubilados	*young and old*
los Juegos Olímpicos (JJ. OO.)	*Olympic Games*
los países en desarrollo	*developing countries*

Had a look ☐ **Nearly there** ☐ **Nailed it** ☐

el piso**	*flat / floor*
la planta baja	*ground floor*
el recorrido	*the route (of a race)*
el/la refugiado/a	*refugee*
la revuelta	*uprising*
la risa	*laugh*
el saneamiento	*sanitation*
el seísmo / terremoto	*earthquake*
la sociedad de usar y tirar	*throwaway society*
el sótano	*basement*
el sufrimiento	*suffering*
la supervivencia	*survival*
el voluntariado	*voluntary work*

Had a look ☐ **Nearly there** ☐ **Nailed it** ☐

Otras palabras útiles	***Other useful words***
aconsejable	*advisable*
adecuado/a	*adequate*
amueblado/a	*furnished*
disponible	*available*
en ruta hacia	*on the way to*
oscuro/a	*dark*
reciclado/a	*recyled*
sin techo	*homeless*
subterráneo/a	*underground*

Had a look ☐ **Nearly there** ☐ **Nailed it** ☐

****Watch and listen out for words that have more than one meaning**

Be aware that *el piso* can mean 'flat' or 'floor' depending on context. So, for example, *Vivo en el primer / tercer piso* means 'I live on the first / third floor', but *Vivo en un piso con cuatro habitaciones* means 'I live in a flat / apartment with four rooms'.